C000006264

CREATIVE UPRISING

How to make a living and make a difference doing what you love

George Hardwick

Creative Uprising

First published in 2013 by

Panoma Press

48 St Vincent Drive, St Albans, Herts, AL1 5SJ, UK
info@panomapress.com
www.panomapress.com

Book layout by Neil Coe.
Cover design by Neil Coe and Levi Washington.
Cover photograph by Tom Ingall.
Diagrams by Lissa at LKG Innovation.
Illustrations by Verity at Sketchy Illustration and Design.

Printed on acid-free paper from managed forests.

ISBN 978-1-909623-17-0

Dedication

To the One Love of which we are each a
unique and brilliant part.

And to the Mother, Lover and Daughter who uplift me.

Acknowledgements

I offer my deepest gratitude to the following:

My families from Nineveh, Leamington, 2Quick, FDM, Yes Group, MyBnk, GMMCS, San Diego and Delhi.

To Lissa, Verity, Fran, Mindy, Anna Mason, Scott Dinsmore, Daniel Priestley, Simon Dixon, Chris Hughes, James Lavers, Dr K. Anders Ericsson, Steve Jack, Alastair McIntosh and my mother. Thank you for helping to make the book what it is.

To my teachers and mentors:

Jonny, Mrs Fryer, Steve McGarvey, Nigel Sykes, Harry Singha, Dave, Crook, Bhajan and Uncle Babu. Your inspiration and guidance have been worth more than words could do justice to.

To my inspirations:

Immortal Technique, Lowkey, Akala, M.K. Gandhi, Joanna Macy, Vimalananda, Rabindranath Tagore, Kahlil Gibran. Just wow.

Contents

Introduction

Dreaming gets a bad rep. To call someone a dreamer is to suggest they lack substance, that they are ungrounded and need to get real. However, that's fairly misleading too. 'Get real' rarely means 'get real'. It's more like 'be sensible' or 'take the safe option'. Here's the thing: in today's world there are fewer and fewer 'safe options'. Nevertheless, if you are someone who loves to be creative, and you've dreamed of being able to support yourself using your creativity, the chances are you've already been told to get real, to stop dreaming.

That is why you have this book in your hands. This book is about making that dream a reality. In the pages that follow you will discover that there has never been a better time to be sharing your creativity with the world, nor a greater wealth of opportunities to be rewarded for doing so.

You may not know exactly what it is you'd like to be doing, but you do know that you weren't meant for a 9-5 life. You are definitely not alone. If you're honest with yourself – if you 'get real' for a moment – you cannot deny that there is something inside you, something you know deserves to be shared with the world. The truth is that if you have ever dreamed of a life that is more fulfilling, where you can do work that inspires you and challenges you each and every day, then you are part of the Creative Uprising, and your time is now.

The Creative Uprising is a natural response to the profound challenges and radical innovations that are dramatically shaping the future of life on earth. We are truly on the cusp of a new world, where technology and science will make life as we knew it at the turn of the millennium seem like the Stone Age. If we are to make sense of, and thrive in, this world that is emerging, we will need artists as surely as we will need engineers. More than this, we will need wholesome, courageous people who are passionate about contributing in their own unique way to a shared vision of a better story for all life on earth.

That is the essence of the Creative Uprising, and that is why I have put my all into this book, so that you may discover your unique creativity, develop it into a highly valuable offering and then deliver it where it is needed most, in a way that rewards you and enriches the world.

You are the Creative Uprising. You have a gift to share, and it is time to begin.

PART 1
DISCOVER

CHAPTER 1

A Gift is Only a Gift
When You Give It

Once upon a time, there was a young boy. As the young boy grew up, he realised he had been very lucky. He had been given a gift more valuable than all the gold in the world, a gift that could not be held, weighed or measured. This gift could only be heard. The gift was given regularly to the boy and his siblings by their parents, for the gift was a sentence with the power to change the world: 'Whatever you choose to do, we will love and support you.'

It is a cause for great sadness and for determined, passionate action that too few children frequently hear those words on their journey to adulthood. Because I was lucky enough to hear them often, I have made some very different decisions in my life that have equipped me with practical insights that I dearly hope and passionately believe will be valuable to you and others like you – artists, performers and creative individuals who wish to be able to provide for themselves and their loved ones by sharing their creative talents in a way that enriches the world. This book is my way of paying forward the gift I was given. Whether you're already a painter, poet, chef, volleyball player, pianist, Persian rug maker or anything in between, or you just know you'd like to be doing something more fulfilling and more creative with your life, I have done my utmost to serve you as best I am able. In addition to offering you the fruits of a decade of personal experience as a performance poet and social entrepreneur, I have sought to capture for you the key lessons from individuals who are outstanding in their field and who possess essential, applicable wisdom for people like us.

Now for the Great News

What's so brilliant is that there has never been a better time to be you. Yes, there are wars, famines, economic crises and some seriously dodgy weather, but none of that can take away from the fact that you are living in a time of unprecedented opportunity. Like no previous generation in the whole of human existence, your generation is part of an incredible shift, a shift that will define the course of our species' history for centuries to come. Understanding your role in this shift will allow you to live a life that is not only wholesome, meaningful and rewarding on a personal level, but which also contributes to making our planetary home a more thriving place to live.

Shift Happens

So what is this shift? Being a poet, I call it 'the rise of the rhyme' – a shift from the logical, analytical, black and white 'reason' mindset to one that allows more flowing, intuition and creativity. Of course we need both Rhyme and Reason but, as we shall see, there has been a gross and damaging imbalance that this shift is now correcting. It is a shift that Fritojf Capra calls 'The Rising Culture' and Erwin Lazlo suggests is 'the Reenchantment of the Cosmos'. For Joanna Macy, who is one of the most impassioned and articulate on the subject, it is 'The Great Turning'. Others may call it 'the intuitive paradigm' or simply 'the shift'.

Whatever label one chooses, the essential thrust is the same: the shift is a complete redefining of human values and a total rethink of the goals the human species strives for. We are moving toward a society where, as Clare Short expresses in *Planet Earth: The Future*, 'we cease to find the meaning of life out of more and more economic growth and more and more consumption.' According to Joanna Macy, we are transitioning from an 'industrial growth society', with its gross excesses, economic exploitations and destructive pursuit of natural resources, to a 'life-sustaining society', founded on principles of nurturing, collaboration and an awareness of the fundamental interconnectedness of all life.

Throughout the rest of the text I will refer to this new era that is emerging using the term 'the rising culture' because it is a shift which will encompass all parts of our lives, bringing about a wholly different culture to the one that has been dominant for the last few millennia.

Before the Shift

Before we examine the key role you and your creativity have to play in accelerating this shift, it is worth understanding what came before, so as to be aware of the old mindset that will certainly cause you some challenges on your journey. Our recent past (1000BC-present) has been broadly characterised by the effects of the shift from polytheistic, earth-spiritual matriarchy to a monotheistic, separate patriarchal deity. The result has been a world that is hugely imbalanced, where qualities such as nurturing and cooperation have fallen to the sword of dominion and victory. In the last 400 years this imbalance has reached its apex. Our notions of progress have been understood through the filter of reductionist materialism, whose godfathers were the great figures of Newton and Descartes. The science and philosophy of these two great minds has influenced how we go about making sense of the world. This has been the age of reason, where a holistic approach has been canned in favour of a combination of reductionism and materialism. Reductionism is the erroneous idea that if you can reduce things to their smallest components and can understand those components, you can understand the whole of which they are a part. Materialism is the idea that everything that exists is in some way matter that can be measured and used for productive ends. The result of this dread union is that the natural world has become devoid of the mystery and wonder it had once held for us, becoming instead a lifeless machine, a series of actions and reactions, causes and effects, a vast lifeless body of 'natural resources' for us to dominate and do with as we please.

It is not just the natural world that suffered under this mentality. By allowing ourselves to be disconnected from nature, we became separate from a part of ourselves. Human life was suddenly robbed of its spirit and soul. We were reduced to nothing but a series of random mutations and chemical reactions underpinned by the hit and miss process of evolution.

Never for a moment could it be argued that discoveries of inestimable value have not been won thanks to this approach, but we are discovering now that we have only been getting half the story. We have been so immersed in our study of the conductor's baton – trying to uncover its weight, the composition of the wood and the chemical make up of the paint that covers it – that we have missed the fact that it is only when the baton is in the hands of a skilled conductor standing before a willing orchestra that glorious symphonies will be heard.

This is the change that is happening. We are starting to understand that reason and reductionism can only get us so far and that we must now adopt a systems approach, a holistic viewpoint, if we are to continue making the breakthroughs and discoveries that will allow our species to overcome the challenges it faces. We must understand how and why life is greater than the sum of its parts.

And that is where you come in.

You and Your Gift

This book is built upon a single idea. It is an idea that drives right to the heart of what it means to be human. The idea has two parts. Firstly, that you are unique in all that is, was and will ever be. There will never be another you. The second part of the idea builds upon the first, suggesting that because you are unique in all the vast complexity of life that exists, you have a unique contribution to make to the development of life as we know it. To put it another way: you have a gift to give.

You may be reading this book because you already know what your gift is and are ready to start giving it in a bigger, more brilliant way. At the other end of the scale, perhaps you've always gone through life believing there is nothing special about you, and this book has found you by random chance. Far more likely is that you are a member of that vast tribe within the human race who know in their heart and feel in their gut they have something more to offer. You may not necessarily know what type of athlete, artist, performer or creative person you wish to be, but you know there is something...something you are choosing either to suppress or merely dabble in, neither of which is leaving you satisfied. The aim of this opening chapter is to examine in more detail the idea that you have a unique contribution to make to our world, and to offer insights as to how you may discover it and/or expand it. From now on, I shall refer to that contribution simply as 'your gift'.

The Egg and Sperm Race

To start exploring your gift, let's begin by briefly checking in with what we know about you. Your journey probably began with your father and mother having a grand old time, at the climax of which (after anything from two minutes to two hours) your father shot you into your mother as 1 out of 200-400 million other spermy versions of you. So, right at the very start of your journey, you were already a one in approximately 300 million miracle. You then swam up some warm dark tunnel where you encountered...The Egg. This was no ordinary egg. This egg was the one, out of the other (on average) 399 999 produced by your mother's reproductive system in its working lifetime, that was waiting for you.

Since I'm sure you're familiar with the concept of human reproduction, be assured that I have included the above account for good reason. Two good reasons, in fact. Firstly, the process of the sperm joining with the egg offers a brilliant snapshot of what happens when you start giving your gift to the world. In your life as a sperm, you were swimming around, doing the same as your millions of colleagues. In the world of work, perhaps that means working in an office or doing some other menial task that is wholly unsatisfying. Your gift is the fertilisation of your talents' potential with the seed of your true purpose, but to ultimately give birth to the life you were born to be living, you have to die to the old you. When you arrived at the egg, you-as-sperm literally had to go kamikaze and dive into the unknown. The only thing that was certain was that you-as-sperm would cease to exist. You had to dive into a new life. You had no idea how it would turn out or how it would grow into something bigger and more incredible than words could describe. You just knew you had to dive. So it is with giving your gift, and you will see in Chapter Two how essential and powerful this idea of diving into the unknown is. For now though, just remember that amazing things happen when you have the courage to dive.

The second reason for including the somewhat questionable description of the mating process is to use it as a reminder of just how incredibly unique you are. The chances of you-as-sperm and you-as-egg joining in that moment were approximately 120 trillion to one. To really get the impact of just how incredibly unique you are, let's look at that again...the chances of you-as-sperm and you-as-egg meeting were:

120 000 000 000 000 to 1

Your Creative Uprising journey begins

Just to be sure you didn't miss this point, as if life wanted to guarantee that you couldn't miss the definitive proof of your uniqueness, the fact was effectively printed onto you in a place where you would always be able to see/feel it – on your fingers.

Your Gift and the Meaning of Life

We will be examining the importance of choice and meanings in the context of your gift in more detail later in the book, but at present let us consider the choices you are presented with when considering the significance of your unique fingerprint.

One choice you could make is to believe that the fact that you have a unique fingerprint means nothing beyond the fact that everything in nature is a one-off creation. No two rocks are the same. No two leaves that fall from the trees into the gutter are the same. Therefore the uniqueness of your fingerprint merely confirms how lonely and insignificant you are in the vastness of the universe.

Alternatively you could choose to be wowed – to look at all the life that teems on this planet and throughout the entire cosmos and be wowed that you are unique and alive and breathing.

The choice is entirely yours, but I have just one question for you: which interpretation would make you happier, would make you glad to be alive? If you choose (as I hope you will) to be wowed by your uniqueness and glad to be alive, the next question is 'Why?' Why are you unique? Again you are presented with a choice: to believe your uniqueness is just the meaningless consequence of random mutation, or to believe (as Ervin Laszlo suggests) that you are a vital part of the infinitely beautiful, infinitely complex system we call 'life'. Again, which would make your life more worth living? Choosing to believe you are a meaningless mutation, or that you have a unique contribution to make to life, that you are in many ways a superhero, and that right now the world definitely has need of your superpowers?

The Needs Of Your Gift

The science of human needs offers a further compelling, more personal reason to embrace your uniqueness and give your gift to the world. Anthony Robbins, one of the leaders in the field of personal development, evolved Maslow's hierarchy to suggest that we have six fundamental human needs. As I take you through each need, you will see how they form a firm foundation to support the ideas we have discussed so far.

Our first need is the need for **Certainty** – to know that by doing specific things we will experience safety, security and pleasure. Conversely, the second human need is for **Uncertainty** – perhaps best summed up in the aphorism that 'variety is the spice of life'. After this comes the need for **Significance** - we need to feel that we matter, that there is a reason and purpose for our existence. We also need **Love and Connection. Love** is the ultimate, but if we cannot get that we will settle for **Connection.** The four needs explained so far are what might be called our 'surviving' needs, in that they are essential to our survival and we will do whatever we can, including indulging in destructive or negative behaviours, to ensure they are met. Spousal abuse would be one example of a negative way someone might meet their need for Significance and Connection.

The two remaining needs could be termed our 'Thriving' needs. By meeting these needs on a regular basis, we can be sure we are flourishing. The fifth need is the need for **Growth**; we need to feel we are developing ourselves and progressing. This is closely tied into the final need, the need for **Contribution** – we need to feel we are contributing to something greater than ourselves.

We can use this explanation of the human needs to shed fresh light on what it means to be human. You began being very much *Certain* that you existed and were alive; however, there was an element of *Uncertainty* as to what that meant in terms of how you should live your life. You decided it would be more fulfilling to believe that there is *Significance* in your unique existence and that you had a gift to give the world. It is the journey of giving your unique gift that will allow you to *Grow* and *Contribute* to the world and experience an incredible depth of *Love* and *Connection* with all of life.

The First Step

Before you can start giving this gift that will fulfil you on so many levels, there comes the pretty fundamental first step of actually discovering what that gift is. It might be the case that you are already clear on what your gift is, and you simply want the 'how' of being able to give it in a bigger and more fulfilling way. If that describes you, then take in the rest of this chapter as a way of reinforcing the deep connection you have with your gift and the empowerment you experience through that connection.

If crystal clarity on your gift is lacking, then the starting point is to understand that your gift is the dynamic combination of two elements: your Reason and your Purpose. By 'Reason' I am referring to the reason you believe you are alive on this earth, the unique contribution you feel you are here to make. Your Purpose is how you actually make that contribution. An example might be a dancer who knows her Reason is to 'create art that changes the world'. Her Purpose might therefore be to 'showcase ballet in places where ballet has never been seen'.

It is important to note that as you develop and change as a person, so your Reason and Purpose will develop and change too. However, it is usually possible to find, and very useful to have, an over-arching statement that captures your reason and purpose and articulates the essence of your gift. Having such a statement helps you to stay connected to what you feel is important and can serve as a framework to provide structure for your growth and development. My own example would be: 'The Reason I'm alive on this planet is to help humanity realise its true potential, so we can create a better story of life on earth. My Purpose is to help people and organisations use creativity to transform their present challenges into opportunities for a brighter future.'

Your response to this may be anything from 'smug ****er' to 'it's all very well for you George, but I've got no idea what my Reason and Purpose is.' In which case, let's take a moment to look at how you can cook up such a statement for yourself and can start to change your life by starting to live it.

You'll Know It When You Feel It

The surest way to know whether something is a large or small part of your unique Reason and Purpose is to be aware of how the activity makes you feel. Since I can put it no better, and because I use this quotation so often in my mentoring work, I'll share these words attributed to Howard Thurman: 'Don't ask yourself what the world needs. Ask yourself what makes you come alive and then go do that. Because what the world needs is people who have come alive.' Another way of saying this is simply 'do what you love'. In my opinion, one of the greatest travesties of formal Western education (and there's no shortage of them) is that our education system fails to get our young people to connect with life's most basic, yet most vital questions: 'What do you love?', 'What are your passions?' and 'What would you enjoy doing that would make a difference to the world?' Instead we bore and standardise them to tears, suppressing the incredible, vibrant uniqueness and confidence they naturally possess in favour of readying them for a life on the wage-slave corporate hamster wheel.

Perhaps you are just embarking on your journey into the world of work; perhaps you have been there for some time. I beg you, do yourself a favour – do the world a favour – ask what brings you alive, and start doing it. Whatever it is, it's your gift to the world.

Gifts and Stories

If you've never been asked to consider what you'd love to do, or have successfully suppressed the knowledge in favour of doing what society told you you ought to be doing, you may find it difficult to begin connecting with what would bring you alive. The first step, therefore, in discovering your gift and being able to articulate your Reason and Purpose lies in understanding and tapping into the power of your story.

It has been said that stories are what elevate humans above the level of more lowly animals. Among other things, our ability to project and reflect forward and backward in time, to comprehend realities symbolically, and to empathise with the perspectives of others allows us to be story-telling creatures.

Stories are what drive the human species. They captivate us and inform our actions, both positively and negatively. For years people believed the stories of Phrenology, which allowed them to justify committing untold atrocities in the name of 'science'. Conversely, Martin Luther King Jr. was able to inspire an entire generation with the story of his dream. Newton was able to elucidate his theory of gravitation thanks to his ability to construct a story around the falling of an apple from a tree. The apple falling was the end of the story. Newton wanted to know the beginning, which he eventually discovered was gravity.

In the context of what we are exploring in this book, the most powerful story is yours. Every step, every breath, every embrace, every tear...it's all part of your life story that is told as you live every minute of every day. If you want to live what you consider to be your true Reason and Purpose, and wish to have the impact on others and upon the world that you desire, it is essential that you connect with your story, with the whole of who you are.

The Power of Your True Story

Living the true story of who you are is so important because our world is crying out for truth. We are more connected than ever before, yet it has never been easier to feel lonely and disconnected. With each new manufactured celebrity icon or revelation about fake Facebook and Twitter profiles, we crave more and more to have authentic interactions with our fellow humans both on and offline. This is why sharing the true story of who you are is a hugely powerful thing to do. You give people the opportunity to make a genuine connection with you. Think about it: when you are checking out a new website for the first time, which tabs do you usually click on? If you're anything like me, you might check out some photos, videos or testimonials, but almost certainly you will spend a moment checking out the 'About' page. This is because we have an instinctive need to know 'what's the story' with this person or organisation. Stories are how we make the world meaningful. Names, dates of birth, achievements, degrees: these are merely facts. They are simply WHAT is noteworthy about the person. However, when we appreciate them in the context of the person's story, we immediately have a clear idea of WHO the person is.

Sharing your story is one of the single most influential things you can do. Once people know your story, they will be able to trust you and be willing to support you. If you don't share who you are, then you will be depriving yourself of vital companions on your quest.

Understanding Your Story

What is your story? What do we mean by that? Your story is everything you are. Everything that has gone before, everything that you dream to be. All of it. To uncover how your story can help you to discover your reason and purpose and can help you to give your gift, I'd like to share an idea with you – an idea so powerful that if it were believed and shared throughout the world it would literally change everything. I don't want to short change you so I'll give you the full version: 'Your gift to the world, your reason and purpose, is to do what you love. When you do what you love, everything you have ever done stacks up as the perfect experience and expertise to help you do it brilliantly.'

Everything you've ever done – aka Your Story. Whether you know it or not, your story is the foundation of your assured success. If you take nothing else from this book, I beg you to accept the above idea as my cherished gift to you. If you can be courageous enough to believe it and live it, I can promise you a life that is incredibly fulfilling and, at times, miraculous beyond words. I offer a very simple example from my own life to give you a sense of what I mean.

Until I discovered Spoken Word and Performance Poetry, I felt like a bit of a failure. You see, my dream had always been to be a film star, so at school I threw myself into any opportunity to perform and develop my abilities as an actor. However, at age eighteen, my exam results didn't go as planned and, since I didn't know then what I now know about the importance of perseverance and determination, I gave up on my dream. Fast-forward ten years, and I am giving a poetry performance to a live TV audience of over 7million people...and feeling incredible! I am doing something I love, and it is my story that is helping me to do it brilliantly.

The years of my youth spent trying to improve my acting abilities may not have blossomed into a fruitful film career, but what they did give me was a love of performing and a confidence in the spotlight that has allowed me to thrive as a performance poet and touch the lives of countless numbers people.

'Great,' you might say, 'but what about me? What if I'm not sure what brings me alive? What if I don't really know what I'd love to be or do? What if I've no idea how my story can help?'

If that's the case, it's time to discover the TRUE YOU.

TRUE YOU

TRUE YOU is an acronym that represents a sequence of questions for you to consider, designed to help you to connect with those parts of your life that are most important to you. Your answers will allow you to begin building a picture of what brings you alive, and of what your gift might be. To accompany this book and ensure it will benefit you in a real and practical way, I've put together the Creative Uprising Playbook. You can get it either in digital or hard copy by heading over to www. CreativeUprising.com.

For the most part, I will simply indicate when there is an accompanying exercise or resource to be found in the Playbook. However, if I feel something is of critical importance to your being able to get the most from the book, and that is certainly the case for TRUE YOU, I will include the key elements of the exercise within the main text.

You will find the full TRUE YOU exercise in the Creative Uprising Playbook, or you may want to carry on reading, but have a pen to hand so you can jot down your responses in the notes section at the back of the book.

T is for Talents

Many people think a talent is something you're born with, some innate ability that you either get by winning the genetic birth lottery, or don't get according to how lucky you got when your 1 in 120 trillion conception occurred. As we will see later, our understanding of what constitutes talent and how it can be developed and grown is changing dramatically. For the purposes of the TRUE YOU exercise, consider 'talents' as something of a catch-all word that includes strengths and skills. There are two main things to keep in mind when listing what might be your talents. One, is it a behaviour or activity that you consistently perform to a high level? And two, is it something you enjoy? It is not essential that you enjoy it, but you must enjoy some part of it. For example, in your current role you may do a lot of typing, which you are very good at, but which you hate because you are typing things that are meaningless to you. However, if you'd love typing if you were able to write what you wanted, then typing would certainly constitute one of your talents.

If you are struggling to create your list of talents, you may want to include things that you may not have done often but which you learned very quickly when you did get the chance. You might also cast your net a little wider. Marcus Buckingham, author of *Now Discover Your Strengths* reveals that, 'talent is any recurring pattern of thought, feeling or behaviour that can be productively applied...if you are competitive, this is a talent. If you are charming, this is a talent. If you are persistent, this is a talent.'

So the first part of the TRUE YOU process: what are your talents?

R is for Routines

Any routine that you have, which serves you, may well have a kernel of your gift within it. If you have managed to keep up the practice of a routine, be it going to the gym, eating your greens or regularly being creative, it is likely that there is something within the routine that you find pleasurable. It is not yet necessary to identify exactly what it is about the routine that brings you pleasure. This will most likely emerge when considering the routine in the context of the bigger picture of yourself that the process presents. For now, it is sufficient and important to identify as many of your empowering routines as possible.

What are your empowering routines?

U is for Uniqueness

We've already established that you're an incredibly unique individual. Now we need to consider how your uniqueness shows up in the world. This could be anything from how you like to dress and style your hair through to what you believe about the world, the music you choose to listen to and the political viewpoints to which you ascribe. Obviously we're all a work in progress, and you may feel there are things about you that are unique for the wrong reasons – big nose, annoying laugh, clumsy – but, for now, focus on the positive and neutral aspects of what makes you unique. By clarifying the ways in which you are unique, a picture starts to emerge of what you value about yourself and of how you choose to interact with the world. This can help you to understand the ways in which your purpose (how you give your gift) may like to show up in the world.

What makes you unique?

E is for Engagement

With whom, with what, where and how do you choose to regularly engage? This could be something as simple as touching base with a friend once a week, or it could be something as large as being the director of a charity that promotes a cause that is close to your heart. Perhaps you regularly go to watch your team play football or play an active role in your local religious community. Here, it is possible that you will start to notice some of your routines merging with some of the ways that you are unique. That is fine; in fact it is a natural part of the process as certain traits and areas of your life are highlighted to you. Essentially, engagement is about how you choose to use the energy and time that is available to you. You may or may not wish to consider whatever work you are doing as part of this.

How do you engage with life?

Y is for Youth

What did you enjoy doing in your youth? What were your hobbies? What did you most look forward to between the ages of 5 and 15? What did you do a lot of? What were you talented at then that, for whatever reason, you no longer do today?

Bringing back into your adult life the things that brought you joy as a child is one of the most incredible and potentially transformational things you can do for yourself. In recent years, I have had the privilege of hosting one of the UK's longest-running poetry evenings, while at the same time running a short-lived pancake café. Poetry and pancakes were both things I loved in my youth and bringing them back into my adult life has resulted in friendships and experiences I'll treasure for the rest of my time on earth. As this example proves, the things you were passionate about in your youth almost certainly hold vital clues to who you truly are and what your gift to the world is.

How did the youthful you enjoy spending time?

O is for Outspoken

What gets you fired up? What creates an emotional response in you? This could be a positive or negative response. The key is that you note down the things about which you are outspoken. If you struggle to think of things, ask what your friends or family might say. I remember one of my hobbies was looking into the crazy world of conspiracy theories. Back then, if you'd asked my family what I was outspoken about, they'd have told you straight away, probably adding in that I was so outspoken on the subject that I was a painful bore. For you, it might be politics, economics, fashion or the ill-effects of the dominant patriarchy that cause you to be outspoken. Whatever it may be, don't censor yourself. Just keep writing the causes down.

What are you outspoken about?

U is for Universal

Here, you are invited to consider what you think should be universally true. What do you think should be the same for everyone? It's important to get a sense of the kind of core values you hold, and considering what you feel ought to be universals in our world is a good way to do this.

Do you think all health care and education should be free? Perhaps you feel every one should have the right to unlimited internet access, or you believe the Sahara Desert should be used as a solar farm to provide cheap electricity for the world. Your universals may be even simpler, such as 'every one should feel loved and supported' or 'everyone should be able to experience joy.' Whatever it may be, note it down so that it can be added to the TRUE YOU dots you've been laying down. Don't worry yet about joining up the dots. The important thing is to have as many dots down as possible from which to harvest a picture of your true self.

What should be universal for all humanity?

Once you've completed each section, you've nailed the first step of the TRUE YOU process. The next step is to distil what's most important. To do this, read back through everything you've listed and circle the 3-5 things that you could not do without in your life. Take a moment then to clarify each of these elements by noting down why it's important, what it gives you, and what it allows you to do. Once you have done this, you are ready to complete the process by harvesting your Reason and Purpose phrase. Remember the importance of sharing your story. Your phrase can simply be an affirmation of how you help yourself and others by living what's important to you. Here's an example of a phrase I helped a good friend of mine to create:

'Through personal growth and gratitude for who I am, I inspire myself and others to exceed all expectation.'

At the time, my friend felt he was lacking clarity on his purpose. After using the TRUE YOU process to really get to the heart of what was important to him and made him come alive, he arrived at the above phrase, which he was able to use as a firm foundation on which to build his daily contribution to the world.

This is a process that works powerfully if you can allow yourself a good amount of time to really immerse yourself in it. In the above example it took my friend and I just over two hours to come up with his phrase, but they were two hours he was very grateful to have spent in that way. If you feel you'd benefit from some clarity on your gift, I strongly recommend that you do the full TRUE YOU process by heading over to www.CreativeUprising.com and grabbing yourself a copy of the Creative Uprising Playbook.

Finding Your Flow

One final way of ascertaining how close to your Reason and Purpose a particular activity may be is to apply the Flow test. In his seminal work *Flow: The Science of Optimal Experience,* Mihlay Csikszentmihalyi identifies a state he calls Flow: 'a state of mind or a state of experience that we feel when we are totally involved in what we are doing.' It is characterised by being so immersed in the activity at hand that you lose track of time and even forget to eat, such is the total engrossment in what is being done. There are a number of conditions that help the flow state to emerge. The activity should challenge you and require you to develop your skills and abilities (remember the human need for growth?); it should also be something that is meaningful to you. What activities, passions or hobbies do you currently have which match that description?

If undertaking a particular activity or path helps you to swiftly enter that flow state, it is highly likely that this activity or field of endeavour is a part of your gift to the world. A good test is to ask yourself whether you could excitedly dedicate three hours a day to the practice and improvement of the activity. If you come up with more than one such activity, ask yourself how/ whether they might combine into a single larger pursuit.

The Golden Rule

There's a golden rule to remember on this journey: IF IN DOUBT, DO WHAT BRINGS YOU ALIVE. First Inspiration, then Clarification.

If the exercises so far have borne fruit, you are by now either crystal clear on what your gift is, or you at least have a rough idea of what you might like it to be. Fantastic. However, perhaps you are still unclear. You're not even sure you have the roughest of rough ideas. If this describes you, don't panic;

just remember the golden rule. We'll see in the next chapter that just acting upon what you love and doing what inspires you will generate amazing results.

I would add two things to reassure you further, the first being some sage insights from my friend John P. Morgan, who's an adventurer, traveller and highly inspirational speaker. John always reminds me that '**your passions are grown and your purpose is created.**' So if, at the moment, all you have is a desire to know what your gift is and then start giving it, that's enough. You will grow and create the rest.

Here's the even better news: you can't get it wrong. It's impossible. Though society may try to convince you otherwise, the concept of 'failure' is one of life's greatest fallacies. There is one time and one time only that failure is failure: when you choose to believe you've failed. Why? Because you will have failed to take the priceless nugget of learning that will accelerate you to where you are destined to go.

According to 'society' I've failed, among other things, at being a film star, a UK Hip Hop entrepreneur, a BBC TV star, a restaurateur and a role model. But from each apparent failure I've taken invaluable lessons that allow me to live my purpose of service fuller and more joyfully each day.

So…failure…impossible. Fantastic.

Each of the things I failed at were steps on my path. Never forget that your gift will evolve and change as you do. At the time, those were the steps I felt inspired to take and each step has helped to grow and empower the clarity of the path I am walking.

A Gift is Only a Gift When it is Given

The reason I've taken a moment to stress that failure is impossible is that I don't want to launch into the rest of what I have to share with you if there's even the smallest chance you might feel left behind because you don't feel you're sufficiently clear on your gift. It is absolutely enough that you have the desire to find it, live it and give it, and are prepared to take the appropriate action to achieve this.

But what is a gift? Ask a 10 year old and their answer is likely to be along the lines of, 'It's something you give to someone.' Bang on. If you don't give what you've got, nothing happens. The world doesn't receive the benefit of your uniqueness and you don't receive the rewards you so fully deserve. A gift is only a gift when you give it.

I'll give it to you straight: please put down this book if you have no desire to make the world a better place by doing something you love. If that sentence doesn't vibe with you in some way, you'll be wasting your time by reading on.

Brilliant. It's awesome to have you on board. If you wish to see a better world and be a part of creating it by doing what you love, then there are no two ways about it: it is your DUTY to give your gift to the world. We're going to deal with any possible response you might have to this fact. You might think it's big headed or egotistical to think you can make a difference to the world. Let me ask you: 'Do you like receiving gifts?' and 'Do you like giving gifts?' They both feel great don't they? So the only thing that's egotistical is you denying the world the chance to receive the benefits of your unique gift by not giving it.

Sparking the Blaze

You may feel like you could never make a difference to the world. To that I'd like to offer a somewhat destructive metaphor. Matches and trees. I'm sure you've heard the saying, 'It only takes one tree to make a thousand matches, but it only takes one match to burn a thousand trees.' I don't want you to burn anyone or any trees (unless your gift happens to be as a forester charged with overseeing the 'managed fires' that are sometimes necessary for good forestry practice), but I do want you to keep in mind that if your gift can spark a change in just one person, that in itself can usher in world-changing events, since that one person, thanks to you giving your gift, may go on to be the Gandhi, the Muhammad Ali, the Tupac Shakur of their generation.

There is one thing to add regarding the perception of your gift. Almost without fail we are our own worst critics. You must remember that perfection is impossible. As we have already seen, one of the only certainties is that your gift and purpose will grow and evolve; therefore it can never be fixed or perfect. Furthermore, it is certainly not for you to judge the worth of your gift. Your job is just to give it and let the people of the world make of it what they will.

Ifs, Buts and Doubts

Now that you're clearer on your gift and why you should give it, how do you feel about actually giving it? If you're anything like me, or countless other performers across myriad professions, there are probably some ifs, buts and doubts making their presence known. Thank (insert preferred deity here) for that! At least we've confirmed that you're human. Ifs, buts and doubts are a common companion to those who are willing to step up and share their gift with the world. You should know that you are certainly not alone. Are there still top sports stars, dancers, actors, singers or surgeons who, even though they have been at the top of their professions for years, still get physically sick from nerves before they perform their roles? Absolutely! Worry and nerves are the inevitable by-products of your desire to give your best. Thankfully, just as it is human to experience such fears, it is also human to overcome them, and indeed to use them to heighten your performance. Your doubts will most likely fall into one of three categories: time, originality or impossibility. Let's deal with them in order.

No Time Like The Right Time

You may feel like it's not the right time to start giving your gift to the world, or that you don't have enough time to give your gift and keep a roof over your head and food on the table. Giving your gift is definitely a marathon, not a sprint. Even Usain Bolt had to learn to walk before he could run. Unless you happen to be independently wealthy, with no other commitments vying for your attention, you'll have to start small. But the most important thing is that you start...that you take some action. No matter how unlikely a possibility it may seem at present, one thing is certain: if you do nothing because you feel it's not the right time, then the only guarantee is that nothing will change. So, act. I offer two quotations to spur you on. The first is some lines you may have come across, loosely translated from Goethe's Faust: 'Whatever you can do, or dream you can, begin it; Boldness has genius, power and magic in it.' The second is hugely popular in personal development circles, and will be referenced throughout the coming chapters: 'what you focus on expands'. Let me delve a little deeper into this second quotation using a personal example.

Recently, I've surprised myself by taking up running. I'd always loved sport and played as much as I could, but always hated running, yet for some reason I felt inspired to start. Practising what I teach, I followed my inspiration and took action. 5km seemed a good target, so I asked my friend who is a serious runner what a good 5km time would be for a healthy, fit, amateur runner like I intended to be. My friend replied that I should aim for around 20mins. My first attempt at 5km took just over 40mins. I had a bit of work to do! Knowing that what you focus on expands, I decided to give greater focus to my running by aiming to run three times a week. Within two months I'd slashed my time to 22mins 3secs at the time of writing. Still a little way to go, but an improvement I'm sure you'd agree. The lesson I hope you'll take is that even if, at the start, you can find only ten minutes a week to dedicate to giving your gift, you can still make magic happen. Trust that you will be rewarded for the boldness of your action because you know that what you focus on expands. There is a caveat, which I'm sure will come as no surprise. You have to keep taking action. Even if it can only be a small amount, keep taking action. My improvements in running would mean nothing if I stopped running and allowed my fitness levels to return to their previous low.

You Don't Have To Be Original

Your doubt may be around whether or not you have a gift that is original and worth giving. Well, we already know, thanks to the revelations of the egg and sperm race, just how incredibly original you are. But if that's not enough to convince you, then consider this question: have you ever needed to hear something more than once before you 'got it'? I remember once being at a friend's house catching up over a cup of tea and being shocked to see that my friend was letting her young daughter sit so close to a candle. My friend's response was that she had told her daughter many times that the candle flame was 'hot and hurty', but her daughter was still fascinated. I watched as the infant stretched her finger towards the flame, getting closer and closer and closer...until she got too close, snatched her hand away and looked up at her mother as she began whimpering. Her mother ran the flame-licked finger under the cold tap for a minute, then kissed it better and watched as her daughter ran off to continue playing. My friend smiled at me and said, 'Now she gets it, and now she'll also know to run her finger under the cold tap if it ever happens again.' *That showed me*, I thought to myself.

I use this example to really emphasise that just because it's not original does not make it worthless. No one will give your gift the way you do. The person you inspire might have come across the same idea, or seen the same thing a hundred times, but it wasn't until they encountered the flame of your brilliance that they finally 'got it' and could use it to improve their life.

Impossible – Just a Word

Finally, you may feel 'it's impossible'. For whatever reason – lack of resources, too old, too fat, too thin, too ugly, too stupid, not old enough, not fat enough, not thin enough – it's 'impossible' for you to give your gift. Let's look at the reality of impossible for a moment. Can you really be certain that giving your gift is impossible? After all, 500 years ago it was 'impossible' to sail round the world - the earth was flat and you'd fall off the edge, never to be seen again. It was definitely impossible back then to fly around the world. 'Impossible' is just an idea that is constantly being redefined.

Talen Skeels-Piggins has been told a lot of things are impossible. He was told it was impossible for him to ski, so he decided to represent Great Britain at skiing. He was told it was impossible for him to ride motorbikes, so he decided to get a racing license to compete in sprints and hill-climbs. These feats would be difficult for you or me, but for someoone in a wheelchair, paralysed from the chest down after being run over, surely they'd be impossible?

Talen is living proof that the impossible becomes possible with enough time and determination. He placed 15th in the giant slalom at the 2010 Winter Paralympics, before going on to claim gold in the Super-G at the 2011 European Cup. After injury forced him to stop skiing competitively, he returned to his first love – motorbikes. He now not only competes against and beats able-bodied riders, but has set up a charity to help other paraplegics to ride again.

Impossible is just another meaning that can be chosen from thousands of others. The only thing that separates what is impossible from what is possible is time. In 1800 it was impossible to converse with a friend who lived many miles away without travelling to see them. By 1900 you could go to a public phone box. By 2000 you probably had a mobile phone in your pocket and could call them wherever you were, whenever you liked. From impossible to possible in just 200 years.

Making the Impossible Possible

There are two key factors in making the impossible possible. Firstly, you will need the right mindset. To ensure you have this, you must cultivate patience, persistence, trust and resourcefulness. Trust that it is just a matter of time before 'impossible' becomes 'I'm possible' and commit to being persistent and patient in your efforts to make it so.

If you feel it's impossible because you lack the resources, it's imperative for you know now that success in anything, especially giving your gift, is not about the resources you have at your disposal, but about YOUR resourcefulness. It's about making the best of whatever situation you're faced with and having the resourcefulness to create opportunities where others would see obstacles. This is something I'm so passionate about and feel is of such importance that there's a whole

Chapter 1

chapter on resourcefulness later, but I wanted to mention it now because of how closely it ties in with the second key factor in making the impossible possible: your why.

Your Why is the reason you choose to do something. The late Jim Rohn would always say 'if the Why is big enough, the How becomes easy'. What this means is that the more compelling your reason is for wanting to do something, the more resourceful you will be at making it happen. Imagine it was a windy, rainy day and you needed to go to the village shop two miles away, but your car wouldn't start (if you're a city dweller you may also need to imagine you live in a village with a village shop!). If your 'why', your reason to go to the village shop was simply to grab a bag of crisps, you'd probably just go back inside and make do with an apple. However, if your 'why' for being at the village shop was to meet your child off the school bus, you'd probably start jogging or ask your neighbours for a lift – you'd be more resourceful about ensuring you got to the village shop because now you would have a big enough why. The lesson to take away is that the bigger you make your why, the more assured will be your success at giving your gift to the world.

CHAPTER 2

When You Dive, The Universe Supports You

The Flowers of The Field

In this chapter we'll look at the bigger picture of how the impossible becomes possible. We will explore the seemingly impossible idea that *'When you dive, the universe supports you.'* Really? Just imagine if it were indeed true, that just by beginning to live your love and give your gift to the world, you inspire all of life to support you to do it. It is absolutely what happens, but I know you'd probably like a little more than my assurance if you're going to start believing it.

It certainly may seem a fairly big leap to make, but its veracity is borne out in what we are beginning to understand about the way the human species interacts with the wider universe. Breakthroughs in quantum physics are confirming what Lynne McTaggert posits in *The Field: The Quest for the Secret Force of the Universe,* namely that, 'human beings and all living things are a coalescence of energy in a field of energy connected to every other thing in the world.' What this statement confirms is that what you do affects far more than you might ever have imagined because all life is underpinned by a field of creative energy, of which you are an inseparable part. Consider a pebble thrown into a still lake. The biggest splash is created where the pebble lands, but the ripple effects will ultimately be felt throughout the entire lake. Your gift is the pebble and the universe the lake. What you do impacts the very fabric of the cosmos and leaves an indelible signature for eternity. You are a unique flower of the field, and it is time for you to blossom.

Talking of Flowers

Before giving you a clearer picture of the science that supports this chapter's big claim – 'when you dive the universe supports you' – let me share a real life example of what being supported when you dive might look like.

I met Anna Mason when she was working for Surrey County Council. We were both studying part-time for a management diploma at Warwick University Business School. Much of the course was fantastic, but inevitably there were moments when our attention waned. During those moments Anna would doodle. But this was no ordinary doodling, the kind you or I might do that ends up with deformedly obese stick men, or a caricature of the sun complete with a smiley face. Anna's doodling effortlessly produced works of art that were as close to perfect as it's possible to get with a Bic biro instead of a paintbrush. I was certainly not the only classmate to tell her she should be using her gift.

Anna's day job involved a series of placements in different areas of Surrey's local government infrastructure. When the time came to choose her final placement, Anna knew she needed to be doing something more creative, but she revealed that her 'thinking mind' was only stretching as far as the parameters of 'creative-within-the-council'. It was whilst pondering her next move that she had her first experience of being supported: 'This particular night, when I was umming and ahhing about what placement I wanted…I remember having this thought process before bed of asking the universe, "show me what I should be doing". I woke up the next morning and it was totally clear to me. I knew. The phrase was 'I need to be doing something with my art.' It was really clear and definite.'

There was only one problem. At the time she received this clear message Anna had not picked up a paintbrush for over five years. Undeterred, she did what she could. She took action. Often diving will begin with following through on a single decision to act. As we shall see later in the chapter, diving is not a one off event. It is a constant, daily process where action begets action. Some actions will be huge, others small. Anna's first small action was research: 'I Googled local art classes and the things that kept coming up were botanical art. I didn't even know what botanical art was, so I Googled that.' What happened next for Anna not only shows how powerfully you are supported when you dive, but also confirms the idea that one of the best ways to recognise your gift is by how it makes you feel.

'As soon as I saw the sorts of images, these very exact water colours…I just knew. It sounds so arrogant, but I just knew I could do better. I got quite excited because it appeared people were making a living from it. There was this excitement, this buzzy energy of "Yes, this is what I should be doing" … I remember thinking, "Well, this is ridiculous! If you have this feeling you absolutely owe it to yourself to fully pursue this."'

Pursue it is exactly what Anna did. Eighteen months after first discovering that botanical art existed, she was awarded the Royal Horticultural Society's Gold Medal and Best in Show awards for her paintings of the apple tree in her garden. Throughout our interview Anna frequently gave voice to her amazement at how she had been supported to live her dream; from part-time work being offered just when she required more time to dedicate to painting; to her paintings earning – to the pound – the exact amount of money she needed to keep up with mortgage payments; even to moving in to a new house in the same village as her framer, which saved her countless hours of ferrying newly framed paintings up and down the A3.

Anna sums up how it feels to be so supported as follows: 'If I'd tried to orchestrate it all, I could never have made it work like this.' Her words echo those of many others I've come across who have been brave enough to start giving their gift and have benefited from 'miraculous' turns of events as a result.

What's the Bleepin Secret?

What lies beneath Anna's remarkable story? Perhaps the best place to start gathering our evidence is to answer the following question: 'What's the bleepin' Secret?' If you have watched either of them, you may have spotted in my rather strangely-phrased question a subtle reference to very popular films *The Secret* and *What The Bleep Do We Know?* Each of these films uses a docu-drama-style presentation to introduce viewers to the ideas of a concept called 'the law of attraction'. Simply put, the idea is that like attracts like – if we focus our actions and energies on the things we'd like to have happen in our lives, sure enough those things will manifest, usually sooner rather than later. There is of course a flip-side to this. If we focus on debt, loneliness or negativity, then the law of attraction holds that this is what will show up in our lives.

Building on the success of the films mentioned above, an entire industry has sprung up around the idea that through our thoughts, words and actions we create the lives we want to live. This is what is happening when you dive into living and giving your gift. By taking action you are saying to life 'This is what I want.' Life responds by helping you to make it happen. However, I don't want you simply to accept my opinion as gospel, and I am all too aware that there are more and more snake-oil salesmen offering flashy-sounding courses and systems based on the law of attraction that are high on talk and very thin on walk.

To put you fully in the picture, therefore, I want to share with you some of the more robust recent findings on this topic. In the last 25 years, as the rising culture has gathered pace, the world of science has begun to discover incredible and exciting new landscapes. The reason this is so exciting is because cutting edge quantum physics is beginning to empirically prove what some of the world's greatest ancient teachings and philosophies have been saying for thousands of years – namely, that we are all connected to each other and to all of life by a web energy that underlies all things. We are entering the epoch where it can truly be said that science and spirit are one; in fact, they have always been. It was just that a different language was being used to describe the same phenomena.

How is this relevant to you and to the giving of your gift to the world? Well, in addition to the discovery that we are wholly interconnected and interdependent, like individual droplets making up a vast cosmic ocean of existence, from which springs the infinite variety of life, it has been proved that the animating force of this ocean/energetic field is consciousness. Our attention and intention have been proven to influence both ourselves, and the world we live in.

The Power of Thought

For proof of this we need look no further than Masaru Emoto's amazing experiments with water. Emoto is a Japanese author and researcher whose studies focus on the idea that our thoughts can have a real impact on the physical world. To test this, Emoto took various samples of water and labelled them with either positive or negative messages and had research participants send the same messages to the water using their thoughts. He then froze the samples and took photographs of the ice crystals that formed. The samples given positive messages created beautiful geometric crystals, while those given negative messages in most cases failed to form any pattern at all in their crystals, or else created horribly distorted uneven shapes.

Spare the Guinea Pigs

Not only do these results offer confirmation that your thoughts can influence matter, but given that your body is made of around 70% water, I hope they also make you think twice before being so negative about yourself. An even more thought provoking example is found in the work of the late Professor Elmer Gates. Gates wanted to test the ability of thoughts to create chemical changes in the body, so he injected condensation from the breath of a man thinking hateful thoughts into the veins of a guinea pig. The unfortunate animal died within a few hours. As he continued his experiments, the results he obtained led Prof. Gates to conclude that enough poison 'would be eliminated in one hour of intense hate, by a man of average strength, to kill perhaps four-score persons'. You may have heard the saying, which it is thought originally derived from the Alcoholics Anonymous movement, that 'anger is like drinking poison and expecting the other person to die'. It would seem this is truer than anyone might have imagined.

The Light of the Mind

Two experiments conducted in the 1980s on the phenomenon of Remote Viewing may literally 'shed some light' on exactly how our minds are able to influence matter. Remote Viewing is the idea that humans can develop the ability to view objects by accessing the information via the source field of energy that connects all things. This phenomenon was popularised by the film *The Men Who Stare at Goats*, and it is known that the technique was successfully used by those on both sides of the Cold War to identify the location of missile silos and underground bases.

In the experiments in question, a group of Chinese and a group of American scientists wanted to understand what was happening at a physical level when the phenomenon was occurring. To do this, they set up an experiment with a remote viewing target – a complex alphabetical character in the Chinese example and a slide of film in the American – held in a completely shielded room, monitored by very sensitive light-detecting equipment. Incredibly, both experiments found that when the target was being remote-viewed by the viewer in a completely separate location, the number of light photons in the room containing the target surged to way beyond the normal background levels.

The significance of this finding has to do with the nature of photons. A photon is an elementary particle – it cannot be divided into smaller particles – and as such, it is one of the building blocks of the universe. The strange thing about a photon is that it can behave either as an immaterial wave, or as a material particle. What the above experiment suggests is that our consciousness can actually bring photons into a particle state – that we can create a material reality from what was previously only a potential possibility. The implications of this for allowing you to dive into creating a life where you are rewarded for giving your gift are astounding.

Making it a Reality

However, knowing the above will be of little use to you if you have no practical insights into how you can use these findings in your day-to-day life to help you live and give your gift. To get the answers you need, I sought out and interviewed one of the leading voices at the cutting edge of this emerging field. Steve Jack is a former Physical Training instructor who spent four years learning the ground-breaking healing techniques of Barbara Brennen as well as adding to his knowledge by studying under Peruvian shamans in the Amazon jungle. The result is a synthesised body of knowledge that is changing lives. I have personally witnessed him, in just five days, cure a woman who had been unable to sit down for six months due to a back condition, without using any pills, surgery or invasive manipulations.

The Practice of Co-Creation

Jack reveals that the reason the universe supports you when you dive is because, 'the earth is going through its own evolution, just like us.' Therefore, if we can master some very basic principles, we can share in an incredible process of co-creation. At the deepest level Jack teaches that, 'The energy field that people know as an aura or that people know as a field of some description, is constantly being emanated as the sum total of all their thoughts, their feelings, their beliefs.' The key is feelings, because how you feel creates your 'energy signature' and the universe 'will be sending in particles of energy to that signature that are an exact match.'

In order to ensure the universe is sending the right particles of energy (which will show up in the form of opportunities) your way, it is vital that 'Whatever you're working on, you have to be able to use your imagination to go to the place where this thing was already complete.' Visualising and feeling in this way will bring you into alignment with where you desire to go, meaning that you will begin to co-create it into existence.

Jack offers three daily actions to help you turn this game-changing theory into a profoundly powerful reality:

1. 'Be centred, master your own personal energy on a daily basis. Don't project into the future or come from the lens of the past, or let other people influence you.'

2. 'Start each day by building the frequency in your own personal field that matches the goal, the outcome or intention already complete.'

3. 'Feel your way through life, live in the heart and be able to feel your way into situations rather than think about them analytically because it's the feeling that gives you the direction not the thought process.'

Steve Jack's wisdom offers fantastic insight into how you can set yourself up each and every day to co-create the life you want in joyful harmony with the universe. He would be the first to remind you that in addition to visualising the successful completion of what you seek and feeling what that would be like, you must take action. During his playing days, David Beckham could have visualised the ball cannoning into the back of the net, and could have imagined what that would feel like as much as he wanted, but at some point he'd have to step up and actually kick the ball.

Active Co-Creation

Without the set-up, the ball will find the target very rarely, but when set-up and execution are aligned, the results are usually worth celebrating. Think of it like two bus stops on a road. If you communicate the appropriate thoughts and feelings to the universe, the universe will ensure opportunity heads your way, but it may be that opportunity only gets as far as bus stop A and you're at bus stop B. Therefore you'd better make sure you're prepared to get your arse in gear and get to bus stop B so that you can make the most of the opportunity; that is co-creation in action.

Knowing What to Look For

If you're to successfully dive and become a master co-creator, you might want to consider altering a commonly used word in your vocabulary. 'Coincidence' suggests a random, chance occurrence. However, if you are successfully co-creating, you will find that these 'coincidences' increasingly seem less and less random. If you know what to look for, you will begin to see that you are constantly being presented with opportunities in the form of synchronicities.

The term Synchronicity was first coined by renowned psychologist Carl Jung and, in its simplest terms, it refers to a meaningful coincidence. Synchronicities are the hallmark of the co-creation experience. They are how the universe supports you, presenting you with the seeds of an opportunity that it is up to you to spot and act upon. By following your inspiration, by living your reason and purpose and giving your gift to the world, you will be serving all life as only you can. Not surprisingly, you will be supported to do this and you will find that more and more synchronicities show up to confirm you're on the right path. Keep following them! No matter how crazy they may seem. Every time you experience a coincidence that seems too crazy for words, and which seems to offer a particular meaning and course of action, do it.

The crazy synchronicities that will come your way once you dive are the universe's way of helping you out. You will never be forced into a course of action. Life will simply present you with an incredible moment that holds within it the potential for an amazing opportunity to unfold. It is up to you to take that seed, to nourish it and to choose to let it blossom through you.

Having the Courage to be Courageous

So far in this chapter we've discovered some of the science and spirit of why and how the universe will support you when you dive into life and start to live your love and give your gift. Now let's look at the more human reality of how and why you will be supported when you dive. Without doubt, to dive takes great courage. Therefore, to find the courage to dive, first we must understand what courage truly is, so that you may find it in yourself and use it.

We will be engaging with two definitions of courage. Both are essential if you are to dive successfully. Courage as we traditionally understand it is fairly synonymous with bravery. Why is this important to your success? Because you will have to be brave in the face of doubts from within and without. This is not a probability. This is a certainty. Others will doubt you, and, without doubt, you will doubt you. You must remain courageous and stay the course. If you can do this, you will find courage as bravery bestows a further gift: support. Only in the very rarest circumstances are people able to achieve their dreams without the help of others and there are few things that galvanise support more effectively than courage. When people see that you are brave enough to do what must be done, no matter the odds, they will be uplifted by your courage and will rally to support you.

The second definition of courage that we need to embody is much older, but was introduced to me through the very modern medium of a TED talk. In June 2010 Brené Brown gave a TED talk entitled *The Power of Vulnerability.* Her talk was moving, funny and insightful, and it very quickly went viral. However, it was the first five minutes of her presentation that held me utterly transfixed. She began by talking about courage, revealing that the English word 'courage' derives from the latin 'cor', meaning heart. Brown reveals that the original definition of courage was 'to tell the story of who you are with your whole heart'. We have already touched on the importance of stories, and this definition of courage beautifully reinforces the point.

Courage Makes a Great Plan B

This deeper understanding of courage is so important because if you can be courageously (bravely) courageous (telling the story of who you are with your whole heart), you will see phenomenal results. Just ask Ben Drew. For those who don't know to whom I am referring, Ben Drew is better known by his stage name Plan B. He is a musician, actor and filmmaker, who broke into mainstream awareness with his album *Who Needs Actions When you Got Words.* It was a pure, straight-up Rap/Hip Hop album, whose 14 tracks contained some of the rawest, in your face, most brutally honest lyrics ever committed to wax.

His next album was as different from its predecessor as it's possible to get. *The Defamation of Strickland Banks* saw Drew demonstrating that he could croon with the best of them, as he let his singing talents shine on powerful ballads such as *She Said.* The reaction to the pre-release single saw the critics and cynics sharpening their knives, ready to tear the artist to shreds for making what they assumed must be a commercial decision by Drew and/or his record label designed to sell more records.

However, with the release of the album and through the interviews that accompanied its promotion, it became clear that the change of style was certainly no money-grubbing, Simon Cowell type scheme. Rather, it was a hugely talented individual making the courageous decision to let his art tell the story of who he was with all his heart. The outcome was that, instead of being widely lambasted, Plan B was almost universally praised for his courage and no small amount of talent.

It was a hugely risky move, but, because of his authenticity, his courage won over those who were ready to slate him. Plan B's example is particularly insightful in demonstrating the need for you to be courageous when giving your gift to the world. Just like the early critics of Plan B's second album, there will be people who are ready to pour scorn on your efforts to live what you love. They may even be members of your own family, perhaps with their own ideas and expectations of what they think is 'right for you'. However, if you are fully committed to telling the story of who you are with all your heart, you will magnetise new fans and supporters who will be inspired by the courage you are showing to do what brings you alive. More often than not you will win over those who doubted you. If not, it is likely their opinion will cease to hold any kind of importance to you as you continue to walk the path of a life that truly fulfils you.

A quick 'heads up' to finish this section. From now on, whenever I refer to being courageous, I mean it in both senses at once – being brave and telling the story of who you are with your whole heart. I was overjoyed when I discovered the second meaning, and I hope it will inspire you to always be courageous.

Knowing Why You MUST Dive

'Our deepest fear is not that we are inadequate. Our deepest fear is that we are powerful beyond measure. It is our light, not our darkness that most frightens us. We ask ourselves, Who am I to be brilliant, gorgeous, talented, fabulous? Actually, who are you not to be? You are a child of God. Your playing small does not serve the world. There is nothing enlightened about shrinking so that other people won't feel insecure around you. We are all meant to shine, as children do. We were born to make manifest the glory of God that is within us. It's not just in some of us; it's in everyone. And as we let our own light shine, we unconsciously give other people permission to do the same. As we are liberated from our own fear, our presence automatically liberates others.'

I'm sure you've come across the above quotation, either through Nelson Mandela, the film Coach Carter, or via any one of the innumerable personal development gurus out there who frequently share it with the world in their blogs and videos. There's a very simple reason why it's so popular. It's awesome, it's powerful, it's moving and it inspires you to remember your unique greatness. I challenge anyone to read it and not feel better about themselves. In the context of this chapter, I'd like to focus on the last two sentences: *And as we let our own light shine, we unconsciously give other people permission to do the same. As we are liberated from our own fear, our presence automatically liberates others.*

I stated earlier that those who may be most ready to pour scorn on you and cause you to doubt might well be those closest to you – members of your family, or your cherished friends and co-workers. Almost without exception their reaction will be caused by one of two things: jealousy or fear. Sorry, but it's true. It doesn't make them less of a person (who hasn't been jealous or fearful at some point in their life?), nor does it make them pitiful specimens, worthy of your contempt. It simply means they are human and are deserving of your love. They will be jealous of you (and they may not even be consciously aware of it) because they wish they had the courage to be as courageous as you.

They may be fearful for a number of reasons. They may feel they have your best interests at heart, genuinely fearing that you will in some way be damaging your future. However, they are not you, and you of course know that nothing could enhance your future more than doing what brings you alive. The other most likely source of their fear is that they will fear they may lose you – that as you embark on the journey of living your love, you will forget them or move away from them emotionally or physically. There is no sugar-coating this. It's very possible, but you know that if they are someone who truly enriches your life and helps you to make the world a better place, then no distance or time could ever lessen how greatly you value them. However, if your closeness is based more on circumstance and geography, then it is very possible that as you grow into your gift, they may cease to be such a strong presence in your life, no matter how nearby they live. Either way, their fear should not impinge on your commitment to dive.

By staying true to what you know you must do and not rising to anger or sadness at their jealousy or fear you will be giving them the greatest of gifts. They will see that if you can find the courage to dive, then they too are more than capable of it. Examples of courageous people such as Gandhi, William Wallace or Erin Brockovich are all well and good, but because society has put such individuals on a pedestal, people can still find the excuse that there is something special about them, that they have something normal people don't, and therefore they could never find such courage in themselves. However, when you step up, as someone with whom they have shared meals and laughter and moments that will live long in their memory, there is nowhere left for them to hide. They can no longer deny the truth: that like you, they too can be more and they too can soar. By finding the courage to dive, you will not only be changing your life; you will be the wind beneath their wings too.

On Gifts and Giving

Your diving liberates others to dive. What an incredible gift. We know a gift is only a gift when it is given. And now you can see this goes beyond the unique blend of talents that make up your gift. It becomes clear that not only do you have a gift that will enrich the world, but that the very act of courageously diving into giving that gift is in itself a gift, for your act of giving will inspire others to dive and start giving theirs.

So dive, be courageous and give gifts far beyond your own.

Take It From Me

Whether you choose to believe it or not, when you dive you will inspire others. One of the most common things people say to me when they ask me about what I do is, 'That's so inspiring'. I'm not a millionaire. I've had no 15 minutes of fame, I've not invented something that's changed the world and nor do I own a company that is a household name. I just tell people that I try to serve people and planet by doing what I love. That's it. I have a longer answer if people want one, but I don't try and come up with a fancy answer just because I think people will want to hear it. I simply tell the truth. And people are grateful. I don't know what it says about the world that we live in, that simply being authentic and true is inspiring, as surely it should be the norm, but right now perhaps it's not, so I invite you to dive and be an inspiring example of truth.

On the Wings of 'What If'

We have covered how others may react to your attempts to dive. We have seen that having the courage to dive anyway in the face of their jealousy or fear is one of the most amazing gifts you can give. But what about how *you* react to the prospect of diving? I can offer you as much extensive evidence and rationale as to why you should dive as possible, but if you are still coming up with reasons to stay grounded, nothing I offer will have any impact. There is one question more than any other that is liable to leave your gift ungiven: 'What If?'

We've established that you are an amazingly talented and wise individual. So the problem is that when someone of your calibre asks 'what if?' your brain will provide you with dozens of compelling answers. The issue here is that almost exclusively we ask 'what if?' with the unspoken assumption that, as you might say, the fit will hit the shan. Ninety-nine times out of a hundred the words we put after 'what if...' will imagine a negative outcome. Have the courage to try something different. Any time you find yourself asking what if, by all means indulge in a brief imagining of a negative possibility, but counter it's co-creative impact by imagining at least two fabulous 'what-if' outcomes.

What If You Build Together?

If you have a family, one of the most powerful 'what ifs' you are likely to have to deal with is 'What if I can't support my family?'

Only an idiot would dismiss this question as unimportant, but it would be unwise to give it so much power that it inhibits you from undertaking a course of action that could change your life, and the lives of those you love, for the better. To resolve this 'what if', keep this saying in mind: 'Let your what ifs become wings.' This will help you to remember the lesson I took on this subject from a film called *Up in the Air*.

In *Up in the Air* George Clooney plays a professional firer. He works for a company who is paid by other companies to fire their employees. Overall, the film for me was a solid 7 out of 10, but there was one moment in it which shone like a beacon. Clooney's character is faced by a soon-to-be-unemployed father who is angrily asking how he'll be able to break the news to his kids.

Clooney's character responds with a question that seems very unrelated, asking the man why children love athletes. The man makes a glib reply, to which Clooney responds, 'because they follow their dreams'. He then asks the man at what point he gave up on his dreams. The man looks at him blankly, so Clooney continues by pointing out that before the man came to work for the company that is now firing him, he had trained as a chef. He asks the man how much the company first paid him to make him give up on his dreams. The man simply smiles ruefully and confirms he was first paid £27 grand to give up on his dreams.

Clooney finishes the exchange by telling the man to seize the opportunity that now presents itself, if not for himself, then for his kids, implying that his kids will not only adapt easily to the tighter purse strings, but they will actually respect their father even more and support him if he is courageous enough to shoot for his dreams. This notion holds true for any loved ones who will be affected as you dive into living your love. If you involve them in the journey and seek out their advice and support, they will hold you in the highest esteem, will take pleasure in helping you to shoot for the stars and, more than likely, they will be inspired to pursue their passions and inspirations thanks to your example.

Taking a 'What If' Walk

If you are struggling to move beyond the 'what ifs', try this odd-sounding, but surprisingly powerful exercise. Make a list of all the 'what ifs' that are threatening to overwhelm you, then give the list to a friend as you go for a walk. Your friend will then ask you all the 'what ifs' on the list, and your job is to respond to them in an appropriately empowering way.

To help you do this, you will not be answering as yourself and your friend will not be addressing you as you. Instead, you must adopt the persona of someone you admire in your field. For a businessman, you might become Sir Richard Branson. If you were having challenges as a film-maker, you might become Steven Spielberg. You must stay in character and your friend must always begin each question by addressing you in character, along the lines of 'But, Sir Richard, what if.....' or 'Mr Spielberg, what if...'.

I think you'll be pleasantly surprised at and grateful for the responses you come up with.

What It Means To Dive

Having spent some time understanding why it's important to dive and how you will be supported when you do, let's close this chapter by looking at what it actually means to dive.

Diving is not a one-off moment, a singular act. True, there may well be one pivotal moment, such as the first time someone pays you for doing what you love, or perhaps the moment your new website goes live, but for each moment like this, there will have been hours of background work to get everything ready. The professional athlete earns his/her crust by performing well in competition, but it is the hours of graft in training that create a winning performance.

Clearly then, diving into living your love and giving your gift is a daily, even hourly act. Passions are grown and purposes are created. Every day and every hour you spend giving yourself to giving your gift is time that contributes to the growth of your passions and the creation of your purpose. Every time you take a risk or act in spite of fear to pursue the sharing of your gift with the world, you dive...and the universe will support you.

Your Still Small Voice

Just as surely as you will be supported when you dive, it is certain that you will face challenges on the journey of giving your gift. In the face of such challenges, given the effort that can be required, and the amount of strategies and deadlines you will have to juggle, it can be easy to feel lost. Thankfully, you came pre-equipped with a guidance system: your intuition.

One consequence of reducionist materialism is that primacy was given to the mind as the seat and source of all intellect. The emotions and instincts were things to be controlled and rationalised away. The upshot of this has been the denigration of the intuition to the point where if you speak about it, let alone act from it, you're regarded as illogical at best, and more likely away with the fairies in la-la land. If the mind was the dominant force in our reasoning, you would expect that the mind would send messages to the heart and the rest of the body in order to coordinate our moment to moment interaction with the world.

We now know that in fact this is not the case. The first place we start to make sense of the signals we receive from the outside world is in the heart, which then sends its feedback to the mind so the signals can be decoded into messages we can understand. It gets even more unexpected. Have you ever had a 'gut feeling' about something, or have you ever 'known in your heart' that you had to do x instead of y? Turns out this is more than just a turn of phrase. Amazingly, your heart and your gut contain the same neural cells as are found in your brain.

As the rising culture continues to confirm that we are each unique, interdependent parts of a vast interconnected energetic web of life, these new revelations about the brain cells in our heart and gut take on a whole new significance. Far from being something to you should just ignore, that little voice you hear may be the purest, most truthful and most valuable response to the moment that is available to you, before your mind, which has been so well-trained to reason and reduce, can rationalise away what your heart/gut is telling you.

Your Path With Heart

Being aware of the wisdom of the heart, and being able to actually following its promptings are two very different things. If you are between the ages of 16-126, it is likely you went through a standardised Western education system. Never was there a better way of training you not to hear the guidance of your heart invented. Slagging off the education system can be saved for another book. But we do need to understand that it will not always be easy for you to hear your heart and even harder to trust its guidance and let it lead you.

What is needed then are some additional ways to help you stay on your path and keep diving. I spoke earlier in the chapter about the significance of synchronicities, and these are certainly the most clear signposts to follow if you happen to miss the sat-nav voice of your heart. If you can make a conscious commitment to heed the guidance of your heart and to follow where the synchronicities seem to point, your life will become magical moment after magical moment of poetry in motion – especially if you can supercharge your awareness by setting a powerful intention at the start of each day and reaffirming it as the day progresses. Think of your heart as an antenna, constantly receiving messages from the energetic web of life...your intention can be thought of as the tuning dial. The stronger your intention to walk the path of your heart, the clearer you will receive the messages you need.

Your Mission Mantras

To help you set your intention and remain aligned to it, you may find it useful to create what I call your Mission Mantras. These are simply requests you make to your heart/higher self/ chosen deity to keep you on the path you must walk. They can also be a fantastic way of grounding yourself and getting yourself ready before you give your gift.

I have a daily mission mantra, which I try to say each morning before I get out of bed, and a performance mission mantra, which I say any time I'm speaking, teaching or performing in public (ie, giving my gift).

The label I give to the energy/deity that connects us all is Love, so my performance mantra is: 'Love, may my words be your words, and may our words be Love.' After saying it, no matter how big the occasion, I walk onto the stage feeling empowered and ready to serve.

I share this technique not to be prescriptive, but simply because it has helped me and I hope it may help you.

CHAPTER 2 ½

The Flight of Love

Love. We hear and see the word thousands of times a week. How often do we feel it? Know it? Just as the embedded correspondents and gratuitous virtual brutality have desensitised us to the plague of violence leeching our existence, so we have become desensitised to Love. It is too commonplace. As common as muck…as common as f***.

To bring back the truth of Love, to feel once again its magical presence in our lives, we need only consider that age old conundrum: Love or Fear?

Which Would You Choose?

Why do I ask this question? Because every day, every moment, that choice is presented to you. It may come in infinite shades of colour. It may be dressed in strange clothes. The choice remains the same: needle or notebook, speak or stay silent, stab or smile, forgiveness or vengeance. Love or Fear.

Like the onion, Love has many layers, and many layers within those layers. But all and every part of it is love. The words you are reading are an expression of Love (as talent) in celebration of Love (life) offered with love (gratitude) to Love (you…god… the children…our planet).

I chose Love. This does not mean I am forever free of fear; the skin of my onion still has to deal with the same kinds of crap we all do. The difference is that I have reinforced the skin of my onion with the Kevlar of forgiveness. So, yes, the bullets of fear may hurt when they smash into me – may knock the breath from me by their force – but they can never penetrate to my loving heart because I choose Love.

How Do You Choose Love?

Listen to your heart. Feel your joy. Everything that puts a smile on your face is a feather. Your talents take each feather to create your wings. Your heart knows how you fly. You simply have to walk to the edge of the cliff. There, far below you, the winds of change stir the waves on waters of love. Here is where you truly must choose. Love or Fear. To fear is to listen to that deafening voice that tells you cannot fly. That shouts at you for being so foolish as to dare to dream. To fear is to step back from the cliff-top and let your wings waste away. The only other course of action is Love – to listen to that tiny whisper that tells you were born to fly, that your wings are like no others, and that if you follow your heart you will soar.

Perhaps the first two or three times you step back. The volume of doubt drowns out completely the voice of the choice of Love. But you keep returning to the clifftop. Something true inside you keeps drawing you back. And that tiny voice which tells you you were born to fly has become a little louder now, a little harder to ignore. You convince yourself the time is now.

You leap…The wind catches in your wings and you spiral upward, elated, free. But this is not yet a pure flight. You had to convince yourself to jump, the belief was not quite there. So, after a successful start, you begin to lose sight of why you are flying. You try to fly for flying's sake. You try to perfect the perfect flying technique. Before long what was a beautiful harmony of flight has been lost. What came so naturally now is being forced and you begin to doubt if ever you knew how to fly. The crisis of confidence really kicks in. Your wings are heavy and they flap discordantly. You start to fall. There is no rescue now. Your wings have become weights. You plummet. Faster, faster, faster, before crashing headlong into the rock strewn waters below.

Barely alive, you drag yourself to the shore, your battered, broken, sodden wings dragging uselessly behind you. You vow never to attempt flight again. You know you cannot risk the wounds.

But time is a great healer. And as you return to the life you once sought to be free of, time gradually washes away the memory of your fall, of your broken wings. What time cannot dim is the memory of your flight, of that feeling as the wind first caught in your wings and sped you heavenward.

More time passes, until one day something happens. Something that changes everything. Now you cannot return quickly enough to the cliff-top. Because of what has happened, you see two things so clearly now. One, that you have nothing left to lose. It is flight or die. There is nothing else. You were born to soar and you have come to claim your birthright. You have also learnt that there never were cliffs, waves and rocks. You never fell. You never stopped flying. You just stopped believing, so you created for yourself a reason not to believe.

This time you are wiser. You have nothing to lose. You have given up everything you were ever told mattered and have arrived at the place where the only thing left is your truth. A truth shared only between you and Love. This truth is your wings. They are more powerful and radiant than before. They are ready. You stretch them in the sunlight, feeling the wind dance through their feathers, feeling an unnameable power course through every cell as you reach them toward the sky. You pause. A moment of stillness to listen to your heart. You feel it thudding in your chest. It is ready. It calls to you from beyond the cliffs, bidding you to begin your journey. It offers a final exhortation, words that become the final catalyst you need to hear, 'Let your what-ifs become wings, that the song of your soul may soar.' You know in that moment that all that has come before has brought you here. There are no regrets any more, just an overwhelming and joyous gratitude. So much endured, transformed in an instant of grace into a meaning beyond words. Everything a lesson, everything a blessing. And now you are running. New lands await, new challenges, new ecstasies. The laughter of your soul bursts forth as the clifftop nears. Your wings are poised. You are here. You will soar. You leap...

CHAPTER 3

Burning Your Boats

No Half Measures

So where are we at? You have a gift the world needs. The way to give your gift is to live your love. And you now know that when you dive the universe supports you. You've got the theory in spades. Now it's time to understand what must be done so the theory can become effective practice. It's time to burn your boats. It's time to choose love.

What do I mean by that? The phrase 'burn your boats' speaks of a point of no return, of crossing the Rubicon. It came from tales of Viking raiding parties, where the chieftains, to spur their men on to greater levels of bravery, ferocity and endurance, would burn the boats in which the army had arrived, so that the only way they would ever be able to get home would be to conquer the island they had just landed on and use its resources to build new ships.

It is no small feat to commit to a life where you refuse to compromise, choosing to sustain yourself and serve the world by doing what you love. It is a truly courageous act. It can be more traumatic and challenging than anything else you've done, but the rewards will be YOUR life, lived on YOUR terms, filled with YOUR joy.

Burning your boats is about choosing YOUR Love, listening to YOUR Heart and trusting YOUR Wings.

I debated whether to include chapter 2½, but I thought it a worthwhile story because it touches upon many of the things we looked at in the previous chapter and speaks to much of what we have to cover in terms of burning your boats.

Make no mistake, like the pupa stage of a butterfly's journey, you face a life and death struggle to become your true self. To break free from its chrysalis shell and to be able to fly away, the butterfly must literally give everything it has. If it holds anything back it will remain stuck half-way between what it was and what it was born to be. I know that you want more than that. You deserve to let the world rejoice in your beauty.

Becoming a Viking of Service

Of course you are not here to rape and pillage, but to burn your boats as you must, it is vital you embrace the task of being a Viking: a Viking of Service. The boats you burn are everything that has gone before you that might seek to anchor you to your old life, to your old self. Like the Vikings sending their deceased to the afterlife atop a funeral pyre, any negativity or pain that still hinders you must be offered to a very special fire: the fire of forgiveness, fuelled by the flames of gratitude. Forgive the wrong that has gone before and be grateful for all the lessons and blessings you have received.

Now you march. You have come to conquer YOUR Island of Plenty. On this island you will find the life you dream of, the life you only dared to imagine, yet which you now know you have come to make real. Perhaps you'd like to take a moment to close your eyes and see your perfect life – where you live, who you live with and what you are doing – whatever it is, it is found on your Island of Plenty, and it is worth moving heaven and earth to conquer it.

Time to conquer your Island of Plenty

As a Viking of service, you fight for the chance to serve others by giving your gift to the world, for the right to claim your Island of Plenty as your birthright and just reward for the value your gift brings to the world. As a Viking of service, the opponent you fight is every injustice and corruption that stands in the way of you giving your gift. Every self-doubt, every fear, every sarcastic jibe must quail before your courage.

Knowing Your Enemy

The greatest enemy you will face will be you. Your own fear and self-doubt will shred your confidence to be courageous faster than anything else. If you are to defeat your enemy, you must know your enemy. For this reason, I'd strongly recommend that you complete the 'Crushing your Creative Castrator' exercise in the Creative Uprising Playbook. Your Creative Castrator is the voice in your head that talks you out of the things you'd like to do, that convinces you something's not possible, that gives you a lame excuse to not do something and then convinces you that excuse is the most valid in the world. You get the picture? Sound familiar?

The quicker you can find a way of silencing its damaging voice and bringing your Personal Power Phrase into your life, the quicker you and your gift will benefit. Your Personal Power Phrase is the empowering opposite of whatever words your Creative Castrator most frequently states.

(I know 'Personal Power Phrase' sounds a bit cheesy, but I promise I wouldn't waste time with something that was not going to be of great benefit to you.)

You will find the 'Crushing your Creative Castrator' exercise in the Creative Uprising Playbook.

The World Prison

Not only will you have to deal with the enemy within, you will also have to tackle a world that has been shaped by the sum total of all our inner enemies. Each of us has that fearful inner voice, and, sadly, when you combine all those fearful inner voices together with the patriarchal, reductionist materialism that has been the dominant paradigm for the last few centuries, what follows is a society that functions very much like a prison, complete with its own wardens and invisible bars to keep the inmates from stepping out of line.

The most powerful of the invisible bars within the prison are those commonly accepted statements whose validity are rarely questioned. Statements such as 'That's just the way it is' or 'That's not a proper job.' Whenever an inmate tries to forge their own path and leave behind the world of the nine-to-five, watercooler, hamster-wheel rat race, the other inmates get fearful. Why? Because if that inmate successfully breaks free of the socially created prison of 'That's just the way things are,' then those inmates who watch them break free will have no excuse not to try to liberate themselves. However, they are not as courageous as you and let their fears hold them back. Instead of facing their own fears, they mask them by lashing out and scorning the person seeking to break free, in the hope that if they tell that person enough times that what they're trying to do is not possible, then the escapee will believe them and stop trying to break free.

Harnessing Your Inner Woodlouse

The only way to overcome this crabs-in-a-bucket mentality is to be a loving Viking of Service who has harnessed their inner woodlouse.

What the hell do I mean by that? Woodlice are amazing creatures, but the thing that's perhaps most amazing about them is that they are the only land-based crustaceans. Their ancestors, the trilobites, were one of the most long-lived and successful species the earth has known, but they lived in the sea. Perhaps woodlice saw the evolutionary writing was on the wall and decided to bail out of the sea and give the land a try. Those left in the sea would have tried to dissuade them but, thanks to their bravery and perseverance, you can now find a woodlouse under almost any rock or rotting log you care to turn over. But it all began with the first courageous steps of the first woodlouse – breaking free from how it had always been, burning their boats and conquering their dark, moist, tree-filled Island of Plenty. So go on: be an inspiring pioneer. Embrace your inner woodlouse, burn your boats and set your true self free.

The First Boat to Burn

As you may have worked out by now, if you are to be successful in diving and giving your gift, the first boat you MUST burn is to STOP CARING WHAT OTHER PEOPLE THINK OR SAY. The single most effective way to experience what some might call failure (though of course you know this is just a misunderstood word that means 'opportunity to learn lessons') is to let the thoughts and opinions of others impinge upon your courageous giving of your gift. If you listen to them, you let them become your jailors, whose words are the bars of your prison cell.

The Dog Crap Test

Undoubtedly, there will be those whose opinions you value, and there will be friends and mentors with priceless sage advice about how you can improve your gift and the giving of it. To help you sort the wisdom from the waste of time, there's a simple test I call The Dog Crap Test.

Imagine someone was trying to give you a gift. If it was some money or a chocolate bar or a book, you might take it. Now imagine the gift they're trying to give you is a lump of dog crap. You'd tell them in no uncertain terms that they could keep their gift. The same is true of people's words and opinions. If you accept the dog crap people offer you, your gift will start to stink and you may well go blind (it is known that dog crap can cause blindness). In this case, you will become blind to the brilliance of your gift.

You don't have to take this

There's a useful filter you can apply to work out how valuable a person's words are – to discern the doo doo from the do it, if you will. The filter is made of one question:

Does this person want to see me shine? If the answer is an unqualified 'yes', then their words are likely to be a gift and should be gratefully received, even if they may have some hard truths contained within. If they absolutely want you to succeed, their words will come from a pure place and deserve to be honoured. If, however, there is a modicum of doubt, fear, or self-interest in what the speaker is saying, then you know you may need to apply some salt and a pinching motion to how you choose to take their words.

The Big 'I Am'

Your ability to refuse the dog crap you are offered will have a dramatic impact on how swiftly and effectively you manage to conquer your island of plenty and be successful in giving your gift. Accepting dog crap from people will mean you are allowing the opinions of others to impact upon your opinion of yourself. If people are giving you crap and you accept it, it's no surprise that you start to feel like crap.

If you feel like crap, how motivated and energised will you be to go out into the world and share your gift? Remember you created your 'Personal Power Phrase'. We did that so you would have a dog crap shield. Any time anyone threatens your self-belief by trying to give you crap, you can raise your shield and remind yourself of your personal power.

In addition to using the shield of your Personal Power Phrase, one of the most significant things you can do to accelerate the success of your conquest is to adopt a set of empowering beliefs. We will always be faced with doubts and challenges, either from within ourselves or from the crap that others throw our way. If you can have a force-field forged from a set of empowering beliefs that you know are true, then those moments will not slow you or derail you as completely as if you had no defences.

The key to developing empowering beliefs is to own a powerful 'I am'. 'I Am': the two most powerful words in the English language, because whatever you choose to put after those words defines who believe you are, and who you believe you are will define how you act, and how you act will create the life you experience. Every single second of every minute of every hour of every day, you have a choice. What you put after 'I am' is always up to you. So make it something amazing and then be courageous enough to let your actions speak the truth of your words.

Dancing With Your Shadow

It is important not to understate the challenge inherent in burning the first boat. It can be a lifetime's work, so the time to start is certainly now. Making a commitment to quelling your doubting voice and refusing to accept the crap of others guarantees a vast breakthrough, because you will be living in awareness that it is within your power to choose to believe you are more.

The reason it can be such a challenge is because, quite frankly, our mind has the capacity to be vicious and cruel. As someone who has had to battle with depression and self-doubt that on some days is literally paralysing, I can guarantee that you will be tested. You will have to face up to what Jung called our shadow – the part of ourselves that we try to deny and ignore. However, you can only be fully whole and empowered when you can face your shadow and accept it as a part of who you are. To help you with this significant step you'll find a video to accompany this chapter, created in collaboration with my wife, who is an expert in helping people use archetypes to face their shadow and move through to empowering wholeness. If you're having trouble Crushing your Creative Castrator and are finding it hard to refuse people's dog crap, your shadow may be particularly demanding, in which case I'd certainly recommend you check the video out. You can find it at www.CreativeUprising.com/Shadow.

Where Enough is Plenty

The next boat that must be burned concerns your relationship to the material world – to abundance and 'things'. If you are to give your gift successfully, you must manage your expectations and reality concerning money. If you are someone who believes that you can only be successful and can only say you've 'made it' once you have a house that is worthy of MTV cribs and a medallion round your neck that cost the equivalent of a small country's GDP, then you may be in for something of a shock when you first start giving your gift.

Gandhi said, 'The world has enough for everyone's need, but not enough for everyone's greed.' The world needs your gift and you certainly need to give it. Therefore, by Gandhi's logic, when you give it, the world will provide you with the 'enough' you need to be able to give it. The key word here is 'enough'. If you aim to raise your own standards each day, and always strive to give your gift to the fullest of you ability, then it is very possible that fame and fortune will follow. However, it may be that the domain in which your gift lies is not as ubiquitous as, say, film or sport. If this is the case, or if you are just setting out on your path, you may need to learn to be content with 'enough'. To help you, let's take a moment to explore more fully the idea of 'enough' and how it may offer an experience of wealth and contentment that is broader than mere cash in the bank.

It could be argued that having 'enough' is the key to being truly wealthy: having sufficient money and an abundance of happiness and fulfilment. Chris Hughes is the founder of The Hughes Company, an organisation specialising in helping both companies and schools attain peak performance from their staff/students. In 2011 I attended an event where Hughes spoke on the power of finding 'enough'. His talk stayed with me and thankfully I managed to grab him for a moment to pick his brains more fully on how 'enough' relates to you and your gift.

Hughes emphasises the importance of being aware of the 'tipping point, the line we cross over between what's enough and then what's not just more than enough, but actually potentially wasteful and not necessarily enjoyable.' During his talk, Hughes shared a fascinating graphic with the group that I have reproduced with his permission.

WHY 'ENOUGH' IS MORE THAN ENOUGH

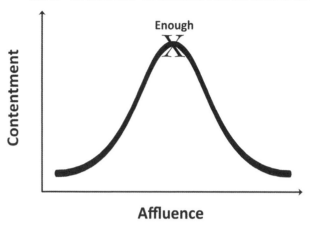

You can see how human contentment does not correlate with affluence in the way you might have expected. Rather than being directly proportional – more wealth = more happiness – the truth is that once we have 'enough' our contentment peaks, before falling off again as we acquire more and more wealth and stuff.

What is going on here? The most likely reason why our contentment peaks when we reach enough is because we are no longer struggling to survive; we can afford to spend time cultivating the things that money cannot buy, but which are essential to our contentment, such as friendship, laughter, creativity and community. Since monetary wealth is not an essential component in these very human contentment factors, we only need the 'enough' that will allow us to give our time to them and feel their beneficial impact in our lives. This human factor may be one of the reasons why we feel less contented, the more we have. Having so much more than those with whom you are trying to connect might cause a person to feel distanced and out of touch with the group. There is also the danger of falling into the acquisitive black hole, where the more you have, the more you feel you need – like a bottomless pit of desire, which no amount of wealth or stuff can satisfy – meaning contentment will always remain elusive.

Hughes is clear though that 'enough' is more than simply knowing how much you need in order to be happy: 'Understanding what is enough stops me driving for more at the cost of other things that really matter to me.' This can be a surprisingly easy trap to fall into and one that can be avoided by recognising the patterns that might sabotage your ability to find contentment. Hughes gave an example from his own life to illustrate the point: 'I was in the Maldives thinking how hard I'd worked to have the holiday and how much money it had cost me, and I realised that if I hadn't worked as hard I wouldn't have needed the holiday and I wouldn't have had to spend the money to go away. So it really seemed like a silly contradiction that I justified spending the money because I worked so hard but if I didn't work so hard I wouldn't have needed the holiday or to spend the money.' To stop similar patterns from playing out in your own life, you'll need to align your values (which we will explore in the next chapter) with the spending choices you make. To help you start making this a conscious process, I've put together the 'Enough's Enough Monitor' in the Creative Uprising Playbook. It combines a register to track the items you'll need, as well as a process designed with Chris Hughes to guide you towards making powerful values-based choices based upon your unique definition of 'enough'.

Relationships Over Payslips

Knowing what 'enough' looks like for you will confer huge benefits. You will be able to develop relationships in a far more wholesome way than if you were simply out for the quickest buck. Knowing your 'enough' will allow you to be at peace with the value of the gift you are offering the world. What do I mean by this? It is so easy to undersell yourself, and therefore always be struggling, having to work far harder than necessary. Knowing your 'enough' will allow you to know how frequently you need to give your gift, and will mean you can confidently request the appropriate remuneration, since, because you are only asking for 'enough', you will know you are offering a fair price.

Furthermore, knowing what you're worth and how it relates to your 'enough' will allow you to feel clear and empowered to ask, give and get: *Ask* for what you want, *Give* where you feel it's appropriate and ensure you always *Get* what you need. I cannot stress how important the cultivation of relationships is to aid you in giving your gift. We will cover this in more detail later, but, for now, while we are on the subject of 'enough,' remember to always get what you need, your bare minimum so you have enough. If, once that is assured, you have the opportunity to give more than you agreed, do it every time. You will be able to build relationships and leave people wowed, and the more you can leave people wowed, the more they will ask you back. The counter intuitive thing in this is don't be shy in letting people know the value of the extra you've given. They won't think you're arrogant. They'll just be even more grateful you gave it to them.

Enough Now...Abundance Later

When starting out, it may be necessary to have a slightly more pared-down version of 'enough' than you might like. I'm a massive supporter of Hip Hop. I think the culture brings something very special to the world. Many of Hip Hop's most famous Emcees seem to share similar tales of having to make do with very little while they were on the way up, so they were able to appreciate, celebrate and share what they had earned once they were at the top.

This is where you will find your gift empowering you and sustaining you. One of my favourite UK rappers is a Birmingham Emcee called Jimmy Davis. I was lucky enough to work with him on his first album and he shared with me his experiences of making the record, which he says were six of the happiest months of his life. For the whole of those six months he lived on an average of £50 a week. He said that far from being a struggle, it was liberating and energising. His focuses were eat, sleep and make music. He knew what 'enough' was and he used that knowledge to help him create brilliant art.

If you do have to make do with an 'enough' that is a little less than you might ultimately like to achieve, it is important to feel positive about the experience rather than seeing yourself as limited or lacking. To help you do this, try to see the times when you have to make do with less as vital investments in your future abundance. Know too that your *value* is sky-rocketing all the while, even if your present *means* may be somewhat meagre. Think of yourself and your gift as a bud. The bud blossoms into a beautiful flower only when the time is right and the sun is shining. There is no use in blooming when it is pouring with rain. Instead the bud waits patiently, soaking up the nutrients brought by the rain and using them to ensure the flower it becomes will be even more beautiful.

Embracing the Squeeze

Like the growing bud, you will not only need to cultivate patience, persistence and adaptability in regards to your 'enough', you will also need to be able to master the ability to 'embrace the squeeze'. No matter how assiduous you are in your preparation or how thorough in your execution, there will be times when you are squeezed. Being squeezed is when you have pressures pushing in on you from all sides. You have no money, you need to spend more time with your loved one/s, you have more deadlines for more things than is humanly possible – we've all been there.

More often than not the reasons for the squeeze may be beyond your control – economic downturn, shifting trends or technologies, or even a postal strike. However, what is always in your control is how you react to being squeezed. Having already stressed the importance of resourcefulness, it will come as no surprise that if you're going to successfully burn your boats, you will certainly need to be resourceful. I mention this now because, just as a personal trainer at the gym will help you to improve your muscle tone and endurance, being squeezed is probably the world's foremost trainer in developing the resourcefulness that comes when your comfort zone is stretched.

Being squeezed is the kiln where the clay of your courage is fired into unwavering commitment and creative brilliance. You never know what you are capable of until you are squeezed. One of my most vivid squeezings occurred soon after I had signed up to a year-long programme with one of my mentors. The program cost £12 500, an amount which I was going to have soon, but which had not yet arrived with me. Then my mentor called and said he'd already committed a chunk of my fee to anther project he was working on, and he therefore needed my payment in the next couple of days. I was definitely being squeezed. Now for some, coming up with £12.5k in a couple of days is no problem at all. However, for me, the most I'd raised up to that point in such a short space of time was about a hundred quid selling CDs on the street.

Remember we covered the importance of developing relationships. I was able to use the good I'd earned through one of my relationships to get a private loan against my forthcoming windfall. That may seem like a simple option but I'd never have thought to ask my friend were it not for the way I was being squeezed. Not only had I paid what was necessary, I'd proved to myself I was capable of raising that much money within two days. Needless to say, that squeezing had a profoundly beneficial impact on what I believed I was capable of from that point on.

Being squeezed is as natural a part of life as breathing. It happens. Just look at nature for proof. Does not the heart contract before it expands? Do not the rocks shrink and the trees grow more slowly when winter's icy grip takes hold? But just because it's a natural part of life, that doesn't mean being squeezed is enjoyable, and since you're in the kind of state where relaxation is near impossible, it's not a space you can stay in for very long without it adversely impacting your health.

It is, however, a space where you can learn invaluable lessons, a space where you can appreciate how the two main types of motivation affect you: desperation and inspiration. All action happens because we are feeling one of these two emotions. We either get desperate enough that we have to act, or so inspired that we cannot not act. When you are squeezed you often encounter both at once – you are so desperate that you are forced to find the inspiration that helps you resolve your challenge.

Based on my experiences of being squeezed and from the testimony of others who have learnt to embrace the squeeze, some common guidelines have emerged to help you use the squeeze instead of being abused by it.

Beware of the Reptile

This means to guard against the reptile part of your brain, which can go on a rampage during a squeeze. The reptilian brain is focused solely on the 3 Fs of survival: Fight, Flight and

Fornication. When you are being squeezed it is easy for the reptilian brain to coerce you into making decisions based on fear and scarcity. However, this is only going to exacerbate the problem because, as you learnt in chapter 2, what you focus on expands. So before making any decision within the squeeze, make sure you check in with yourself and ensure that your heart is guiding you from a place of enough, rather than the reptile coercing you from a place of lack.

Learn to Love the Adrenaline

As stated above, relaxation time will be pretty minimal during a squeeze. Learning to love the rush you get from the adrenaline is important, especially in those moments where you feel so overwhelmed you're sure your head will literally explode. Try to take a deep breath or laugh out loud while setting the intention to let the adrenaline fuel even greater resourcefulness as opposed to causing brain-frying overwhelm.

Keep the Faith, Keep Hydrated, Keep Nourished

Even in the depths of the squeeze, it is vital that you are visualising a positive outcome: what you focus on expands. To help your mind and body to help you, make sure you stay even more hydrated than usual. Since your brain will be working overtime, it will be using far more water than usual, so make sure you keep topping it up. Don't shirk on nutrition either. It's very easy to fall into the trap of thinking you've got to use all your time to resolve the squeeze and therefore taking the time to eat anything, let alone eating well, is a luxury you can't afford. The truth is you can't afford not to. Poor nutrition will sap the body of the energy it needs to keep performing at the levels required to steer you through the squeeze.

If you can follow these steps you'll give yourself the best possible chance of gaining great benefit from any squeeze. Remember, you will be squeezed. Guaranteed. Now I hope you'll be able to use the experience to accelerate your gift-giving instead of letting the challenge overwhelm you.

PART 2
DEVELOP

CHAPTER 4

Get Real: Invest Maximum Effort

The preceding three chapters were focused on helping you to understand your gift and to grasp some of the mindset and preparations needed for you to be able to give your gift. The chapters in this second section are focused more on the practicalities of what is required for you to develop your gift into a world-class offering, one that will benefit and wow the world and earn the rewards you so richly deserve.

If the previous chapters were about why you should take action, what follows is the how – how to take action so that a world-class offering is the final outcome. A quick heads up before we launch into it: this is where the rubber hits the road. The guidance in the following chapters assumes you are prepared to put the work in. A lot of it. Since you are pursuing something you love, you may choose not to see it as work. Just know that whatever you call it, there are no shortcuts and there must be maximum effort.

Getting R.E.A.L

Since maximum effort is required, the first step is to ensure that the effort you do put in is not wasted. To successfully minimise false steps and wasted energy, the action you take must originate from a firm foundation. The key to this is to have a robust and inspiring plan.

Allow me to introduce you to my REAL strategy. Taking inspiration from the TRUE YOU process, this acronym will help you to get crystal clear on the big picture of how you are going to develop and give your gift. It would definitely be a good idea to follow through with the exercise parts of this as you read.

You'll find the whole process flows much more authentically. Therefore, I massively recommend that you complete your REAL Strategy in the Creative Uprising Playbook. If you're not up for that, I'd at least advise you to note your observations down as you go through the following four sections, as they really do provide an excellent launchpad from which to take off.

Your REAL Strategy

R is for Reason

This is your BIG WHY, the compelling reason that gives you the drive and the courage to dive and burn your boats. A good way to begin figuring it out is to ask what makes you 'lose the snooze'. What gets you leaping out of bed energised and enthused the moment you hear the alarm clock?

To give you an example, one of the big goals I set myself relating to my Reason and Purpose was to establish myself as the world's leading personal development poet. I put down three things under my BIG WHY Reason.

1. I love creating inspiring poetry and using it to help people.

2. It is a talent I have, therefore I have a duty to share it.

3. It is me in my flow.

I knew that no matter what might happen, if I kept connecting with those reasons for why I was working towards achieving my goal, I would always have the motivation to persevere.

So go ahead and list your 'lose the snooze' REASONS WHY you are inspired to develop and share your unique gift. If you completed your TRUE YOU, it is highly likely that your WHY will align with some or all of your TRUE YOU statement.

E is for Ethics

This is about making your actions and the goals those actions are working towards aligned with who you are and what you value as a person. Ultimately your ethics are what you will become known for. They will become the foundation of your brand. Moreover, it is likely that when you come to form mission statements and literature that explains who you are and what you do, you will harvest heavily from your Reasons and Ethics as a means of congruently articulating your beliefs to the wider world.

The importance of your ethics becomes clear when you realise that your brand is not your logo. It is the promise you make to the world of what your gift is and how you will give it. Being crystal clear on your ethics and being strongly committed to them will ensure you always deliver on your promise. Moreover, when you are clear on your ethics, you are far less likely to give your gift in a way that is dissonant with the promise of your brand. Consequently, you will be seen as someone people can rely on and the value of your brand and your gift will therefore increase.

Take a moment to list your ethics, which can be summed up as the values and principles you live by that no amount of money would change. If you did the TRUE YOU exercise in Chapter One, you may want to be guided by some of your answers to your Engagement, Outspoken and Universals.

A is for Activities/Actions

Your activities should be you in your flow. They are the activities which will most contribute to increasing the value of your gift and people's awareness of it. They are also the activities that you are happy to immerse yourself in, dedicate to and stretch yourself in pursuit of their improvement. The three activities that fit these criteria for me are writing, speaking/performing and teaching. You may have only one, or more than three. My hunch is that it would be challenging to have more than five such activities and be able to dedicate the necessary time to them, whilst still being able to give enough time to the other things that make life worth living – being a mother, father, lover or friend.

Actions are different. As was stressed at the start of the chapter, there's no more dabbling or half-arsed. It's time to Get Real, Investing Maximum Effort. It's time to identify some actions you can take that will immediately start gathering momentum for your gift giving...and then DO those actions.

Here's the brutal truth. Unless you're lucky enough to have the perfect team and support behind you from the start, you're going to have to do some stuff you'd rather not do and which more than likely bores the hell out of you. This is why it is essential to be smart with your actions. There is a balance to be struck.

To keep you doing what needs to be done, you may want to consider making the more menial actions the filling of your daily action sandwiches. What am I on about? I'm suggesting that for each action you have to take that does not light you up with enthusiasm, but which is nevertheless necessary for your success – such as setting up a bank account or keeping your Twitter updated – try to put these in between two of the activities that do enthuse you and bring you alive. Personally, I always start the day by doing something creative. Then I'll do something that's a tedious but necessary item on my to-do list, after which I'll do something that is creative again. I know that ultimately it is my creative output that will most greatly contribute to my success, but there's no point in being creative if I don't have the systems in place so the world can benefit from that creativity.

If you are struggling to find motivation in your actions, always connect back in with your Reason Why. Knowing why you are doing something gives it a meaning beyond the task itself and can often add an element of pleasure to what would otherwise have been mundane.

Go ahead: List at least three actions you can do in the next 48 hours that will serve your long-term success in some way, and do them.

L is for Long-term

Perhaps the biggest sadness I have felt over the last decade or so is at the short-sightedness displayed by governments and corporations, where the majority of decisions were made based on improving short-term re-election hopes or quarterly balance sheets, rather than acting in a way that would have produced profound benefits for people and planet in the long-term.

You are not going to make the same mistake. You're going to Warren Buffet your dreams. Warren Buffet always said he would never invest in a company whose future success he couldn't predict twenty years down the line. They were his ethics. They informed his actions, and they certainly proved pretty useful. He's one of the world's most successful investors.

There's a quite longwinded, but very helpful question to answer that will help you be clear on your long-term aims and ambitions: What long-term benefits for yourself and others will your ethically-reasoned actions create?

This is where we bring it all together. Your Long-term is the guiding intention you set for the lifelong project of giving your gift. It becomes your guiding star. It's where the ultimate dream is kept. If everything unfolded as you hoped, what would you like to see happening? You do not necessarily need to make vision time-bound. Your dreams will unfold at the pace they must. If you keep taking wise action that is congruent with your Ethics and grounded in your Reason Why, the results you aspire to will be assured.

Think of your Long-term as a magic blackboard. Whatever you write on your magic blackboard will come true. What do you dare to write?

What Long-term aims, dreams and goals do you have around giving your gift?

Investing in Your Success

Now that you know how to get REAL when it comes to giving your gift, the next step is to understand how to invest in yourself so your maximum efforts will bear abundant fruit. In order to get clarity on successful self investment, we need to speak about fridges. Life is like a fridge. You can only get out of it what you put into it. If you choose to stock your fridge with crap, there's no way you'll be able to cook a nourishing meal from what's inside, no matter how talented a chef you are.

However, if you stock your fridge with awesome fresh ingredients then the possibilities of the wholesome feasts you can create are endless. This is why it is essential to invest wisely in yourself. Every investment in yourself is an item you are choosing to put in your fridge for future use, so make sure you are choosing wisely.

In addition to being discerning about what you choose to invest in, it is also paramount that you know when to invest. If you are running a restaurant there is no use investing in more tables and chairs if the ingredients are sub-standard and chef's knives are blunt. The food coming from the kitchen will be terrible and the new tables and chairs will stay empty. The time to invest in more covers is when there is a queue outside the door of loyal customers desperate to taste the fantastic cuisine.

Investments: Make Them EPIC

So what should you invest in and when? Of course there are no hard and fast answers, but you will never go far wrong if you always try to keep your investments EPIC: Education. Products. Infrastructure. Community.

Before I explain a little more on each of these areas, it is worth noting that the nature of any investment is that you are looking for a return on it. Traditionally, this would be monetary, but in your case it may not always be. Nevertheless, it is essential you know what benefit you expect to get back from whatever investment you are making. If you don't keep this in mind, it is highly likely that you will not make the most of the opportunities your decision to invest presents you with.

Education is the mother of all investments. If you can only choose one type of investment in yourself, invest in your education. There is a very specific piece of guidance you should take on board when it comes to knowing how to get the best out of investing in your education. The prevailing wisdom of schools and businesses is that you should focus your training or education on remedying your weaknesses. However, nothing could be further from the truth for the purposes of using education to improve the giving of your gift.

The key is to invest in your strengths. Think about it: a footballer doesn't receive coaching on how to drive a car. He/she works with the coaches to become an even better footballer. Similarly, opera singers are, by definition, some of the best singers on the planet, yet they spend a huge amount of time working with vocal coaches and breathing coaches so that their asset – their voice – becomes even more valuable.

Your gift may be one specific thing, or it may be the combination of an array of talents that manifests as a particular type of expression. Wherever your gift lies on that spectrum, the key word to consider when assessing how to invest in your education is 'synergy' – what area of strength can you improve so that your gift becomes even greater than the sum of its parts?

Products are how the world receives your gift. It may be that you need to hire a venue to give a performance or spend money creating a book or CD. Nothing will help you with time-management like well-created products. They allow you to reach a wider audience than would ever be possible if you had to be there in person each time. It is especially important to know what return you expect from products and what you want them to help you achieve. I have seen so many musicians throw money at getting a CD pressed up, only to see the CD sitting in boxes on their shelves because they did not have the long-term plan in place for how they were going to get that CD out into the world. In time they have moved on and created new, fresher music and the time to share the earlier CD has passed, meaning ultimately it proved a waste of time, energy and money, all because they were unclear on the return they wanted and how they were going to achieve that return.

Infrastructure relates to ensuring you have in place the systems you need to share your gift with the world. These days a website is an example of an essential piece of infrastructure that almost anyone with a gift for the world must have. Know that your infrastructure, like your gift, will need to grow and evolve. Given the pace of technological change it can be tricky to guarantee that the infrastructure you are investing in will continue to be relevant for as long as you hoped, but don't let that stop you. You will always be able to take lessons from every experience, so simply ensure that you are clear on why you are investing in this infrastructure now, and what will be the long-term benefits you believe it will reap.

Community refers to the investments you make to help you build your tribe and cultivate relationships. More often than not, investments in your community will be in the form of time rather than money; responding to emails/tweets/facebook or spending time at events and venues where those you want to connect with choose to spend their time. It can be easy to fall into the trap of feeling like you are being calculating and manipulative if you actually take a moment to be clear on what you want to get out of cultivating a relationship with a particular person. There's a very simple procedure to combat this. It's called caring.

Whenever you approach someone, if you do it with a genuine desire to help that person give their gift to the world more fully, then you will reap the rewards. If, as time progresses, you find you are the only one giving in the relationship, then you know that this is someone who is not worth continuing to invest your time in. If the relationship is healthy, both parties will feel inspired to help each other. Action will spring from a mutual desire to enrich the world. If such mutual inspiration is not present, you can move on safe in the knowledge that you gave from the heart, but that this particular moment was not the right one for you to forge this relationship.

Having such an awareness of relationship dynamics is vital to successfully investing in your community. In essence, a community is the result of numerous one-on-one meetings; therefore, understanding how to foster great one-on-one relationships will drastically amplify the strength of your community-building.

To wrap up this overview of wise self-investing, it is important to stress just how effectively your gift can allow you to invest. More often than not, the investment you need to make will cost money. If you haven't got much, that can be a bit of a problem. This is why it is so vital to be constantly cultivating relationships and to be sharing your gift as much as you can. To give you an example, by leveraging my relationship with one of my mentors I was able to share my gift with two different trainers whose courses I was keen to attend. The result was that for a total contribution of £200 towards course materials I was able to receive over £7000 worth of education. It's not about resources. It's about resourcefulness. If you're lacking the necessary monetary resources, then your gift and your relationships are the two best resources you can get resourceful with.

Being Effecticient
(Or 'How to do the right thing right')

Now you're clearer on how to get the most from the opportunities you will have to invest in yourself, it's time to get crystal clear on how to get the most bang for your buck. Step number one comes courtesy of Sir Richard Branson. Any time someone asks him how they can be more productive, he gives the same answer: work out. Far from tiring you, exercise will give you the energy you need to put in the kind of effort that will be required of you as you dedicate to giving and improving your gift.

Through your REAL strategy, you know what actions are going to serve you most, so here are a few 'learned the hard way' insights to keep you on track as you take action.

Before the made up word appeared above, you had two choices: to be effective or to be efficient. For years the drum of efficiency has been beaten by the corporatocracy as the reason why their way of doing things is the right one. Here's the thing: only effective guarantees to get the job done. There's a small but subtle difference that makes all the difference. Efficient is 'doing things right'. Effective is 'doing the right thing'. When it comes to giving your gift, there will be no end of people and books telling you how to 'do things right'. You must be able to pick through the multitude and find the way that works for you to 'do the right thing'.

Let's imagine an example. Suppose I asked you to paint my house blue. You'd want to know which was my house. I'd tell you my house is the pink house in Spencer Street with a red car parked outside. So if you arrived in Spencer Street and began painting a pink house with a red car parked outside, you'd be 'doing things right': you'd be being efficient. However, you wouldn't be being effective because in fact you'd not gone far enough up Spencer Street to see that there was another pink house with a red car parked outside, which was my house. My neighbour, who also has a red car, and who used to have a pink house, would have been a lot more happy if you'd done the right thing and been effective, instead of efficiently painting the wrong house.

I use this fairly simplistic example to highlight the pitfalls of working for the sake of working. To successfully give your gift to the world you will need to put the work in. Most likely a lot of work. But you'd be better off doing nothing than simply working for working's sake. It's no good slogging your guts out if the slogging is not helping you develop and give your gift.

Inspiration Not Cash

To discern whether your work is likely to be effective you can never go far wrong by asking if it inspires you. Using your daily action sandwiches should help to keep you on track, but it's always of benefit to keep connecting with the golden rule – do what makes you come alive.

Of course there is a balance to be struck. It's no good ignoring the money and starving while you try to come alive, but that is why we spent some time connecting with the power of 'enough'. Once that is taken care of, it is likely you will still be presented with situations where you can act in a way that will bring in more income, or in a way that will bring more inspiration. The choice is always yours, but my guidance is that choosing inspiration is like making a deposit in the bank of life. Remember the bud. By investing in inspiration you are feeding the maturing bud of your gift, so that each time your gift has the chance to blossom it will do so even more awesomely.

When you choose to work on inspiring, you are going to be more energised. This means that if you encounter others as you do the work, you will flood them with that inspiration, which, of course, is going to serve your relationship-building as an additional bonus on top of whatever the outcome of the work will be.

Always remember that there are millions of ways to earn money, but there is only one way for you to be valued as fully as you deserve, and that is to inspire the world as only you can.

Don't Forget The Fun

Perhaps the thing that has suffered at the hands of reductionist materialism more than anything else is fun. Nowhere is fun more reviled than in the workaday corporate world – indeed fun is so outlawed in that world of suits and ties, that to describe someone as 'a suit' is to suggest they are incapable of having fun.

The suits probably thought they were doing the right thing in outlawing fun. Children have fun. Artists have fun. Surely fun, therefore, has no place in serious business. This logic would have been sound, but for one fatal flaw: to remain competitive, businesses must be creative enough to be adaptable. The pace of change is such that those businesses who cannot change or adapt begin to be called dinosaurs, then – like the dinosaurs – they die out. To be creative is to harvest the fruits of the imagination into something valuable, and there is nothing that fuels the human imagination like fun.

However, fun is more than creativity fuel. Fun is human fuel. It helps us to be more effective, more productive and to learn faster and deeper. More than all of these, fun can be your light in the darkness. If you want to give your gift to the world, you are going to have to practise and practise and practise some more. When you've finished, you can celebrate by practising some more and then taking a moment to practise again. There will be times in that practice where you will want to give it all up and forget you ever had a gift. If you've not made a conscious effort to make having fun a part of your practice, then you probably will give up. Making a commitment to having fun and weaving it into your daily routine could be the difference between the world celebrating your revolutionary gift and rewarding you accordingly and you having a hobby that once upon a time you could have taken further. I know that's not a tale you want to be telling, so do take the time to get creative and unleash your imagination on the question of how you can you bring more fun into your practice routine and into your daily life?

CHAPTER 5

Creating a World-Class You

The Truth About Talent

Since your gift boils down to your unique expression of your unique talents, it is essential that you refine your understanding of what talent is and how it can be developed. Much like our understanding of the universe, where quantum physics and the rising culture is consigning reductionist materialism to the history books, our understanding of talent is changing dramatically.

The old view can be summed up as 'If you got it, you got it. If you don't, you don't.' Talent was seen as something innate, literally a gift from God, or a victory in the genetic lottery for the atheists out there.

However, recent works such as Malcolm Gladwell's *Outliers* and Daniel Coyle's *The Talent Code* have begun to shed fascinating new light on talent. Far from being something you are born with, talent is something that you grow, just like your passions. From this perspective the world really is your oyster. You can develop the ability to be a master in pretty much whatever field you choose, providing you are willing to commit the necessary time to practise.

Talent Lessons from an Annoying Ginger Kid

The power of practice was brought home to me one morning when I was shown a YouTube video of somebody I recognised. Back in 2007 I was trying my hand at being a record label mogul. I had begun by being a club promoter and when my enthusiasm for that waned, my best friend and I decided that the next logical step was to take the musicians we had encountered as club promoters and start up a record label that would surely catapult us to fame and millions.

Obviously it didn't work out quite like that, but it was a time full of fond memories and strange meetings. We managed to secure a touring spot for one of our artists supporting a fairly well-known independent band who'd recently had a number one hit. On a number of occasions during this tour we encountered a young guy who, officially, was there to help out the main band by tuning their guitars and so on, but who seemed to me to do little more than swan around star-struck whilst drinking all the free beer that was left back stage.

One night he had nowhere to stay, and, since we were trying to make a DVD to accompany out new record label, we allowed the homeless beer drinker to sleep on our sofa in exchange for letting us get some footage of him performing a few songs. The only other thing I recall from that time was at the end of the tour when we all went to some bar-cum-bowling alley in London, where this young guy got very drunk and kept asking me to rap battle him.

The years rolled on and our fairly flimsy attempt at a record label fell away. I thought nothing more of the annoying drunk kid we'd encountered...until a late spring morning in 2010. At the time I was teaching music in a Pupil Referral Unit and one of my students called me over, telling me I had to check out this video on YouTube.

The next thing I had to do was a double take. There, right before my eyes, was the annoying kid who'd got drunk on tour with us, slept on my sofa and lost a rap battle to me. Except now it was different. Back then he'd been just a 16 year old kid who could play the guitar and sing, but not to the extent that he was instantly captivating. Now he'd just turned 20 and was absolutely nailing it. The video I was watching was fast becoming an underground hit that would make him a household name among the country's teens before the summer was out.

Fast forward to the present day and Ed Sheeran is poised to become one of the UK's biggest superstars. By Christmas 2011 his debut album had already achieved double platinum status and at the time of writing his break-out single *The A Team* has gone platinum in the USA.

So what happened to transform the annoying ginger kid who slept on my sofa into a global superstar? To put it simply, he got good. Very good. You may not appreciate his music, but what cannot be questioned is the quality of his singing voice, his unique musicianship and his ability to spit raps on a par with the best.

How did he get so good? He applied the talent formula.

The Talent Formula

The Talent Formula is the synergy of three essential elements:

Practice, Mindset and Setting.

Practice

According to mainstream popular science 10 000 hours of practice is the magic number that leads to the creation of a world-class talent. Indeed, both Gladwell and Coyle quote the figure in their respective works, but just how accurate is it? To find out, I went direct to the source. From 1993 onward Dr Anders Ericsson has consistently published some of the most revolutionary findings in the field of expert performance. It was his research that served as the original inspiration for what became 'the 10 000 hour rule'.

In reading around the subject I came across a letter written by Dr Ericsson in which he claimed that Gladwell and others had, in coining 10 000 hours as 'the magic figure', misrepresented and oversimplified the findings of his work. To get the real story, I called him up. He was kind, attentive and clearly passionate about his work. Based on our call and the pages of research he subsequently sent to me, I've been able to distil from Dr Ericsson's findings the four rules of optimal practice, which, if implemented, will ensure you're doing what needs to be done to develop your talents in the most appropriate way.

Rule #1: No Shortcuts!

I'm afraid it's true. Even if the 10000 hours rule is wide of the mark, there's no hiding from the fact that you're going to have to make a serious time commitment that will be measured in years rather than months. Dr Ericsson revealed that, before they reach the top of their game, some musicians have put in over 25 000 hours practice.

Rule #2: It's about how WELL you practise.

Both Coyle and Dr Ericsson emphasise that in order for your performance to improve, practice alone is not enough. A chef could practise cooking a steak for years, but they will never have a happy customer if their practice only improves their ability to burn the steak. Instead of mindless repetition, you must engage in what Dr Ericsson calls 'Deliberate practice', and what Coyle terms 'Deep practice.' In this form of practice, you stretch yourself beyond what you are capable of and commit to gradually mastering new skills through very specific, focused attention.

Coyle identifies the need to go from big to small to big again – knowing what you wish to achieve (big), then chunking it down into smaller parts which you practise to mastery (small) and then linking the parts back together to reassemble the now mastered big picture (big). Similarly, Dr Ericsson stresses that 'this type of practice requires intense concentration on improving particular aspects of performance.'

A good rule of thumb for deliberate practice is Why, What, How. Know Why you are practising a specific task (what contribution this practice makes to your overall progress), know What specifically you wish to achieve in your practice (where you are now, where you wish to get to), and know How you are going to achieve it (How you will close the gap between where are you now and where you wish to be.)

Rule #3: Get feedback.
The need for feedback goes hand in hand with getting the most from deliberate practice. Dr Ericsson confirms that 'The design of situations in which individuals can receive immediate feedback is one of the essential prerequisites for deliberate practice activities.' When you know Why you are practising and What you wish to achieve, you will need to know how to refine your How, so that you are able to effectively close the gap between where you are and where you want to get to. This is only possible if you are getting accurate and expert feedback.

Rule #4: Get the right help.
It is nigh on impossible to 'go it alone' and achieve the highest levels of performance and mastery. Why? Because the right feedback can only come from an external source. Usually feedback will be received from another expert, a coach, a mentor or a learning resource that will allow you to receive swift, targeted and appropriate feedback. You only need to look at the progress of Andy Murray to see the power of getting the right help. Everyone knew

he had the potential to win Grand Slams, but it wasn't until he received the right help from Ivan Lendl that he was able to take the necessary final steps to close the gap between runner up and champion.

Mindset

Here, desire and discipline forge an inseparable bond. Your thousands of hours of deliberate practice will be a lot of time wasted if you do not harness the power of mindset to ensure that your practice retains the intensity required. Deliberate practice will, by its very nature, often be challenging and uncomfortable as each day, each hour, each minute you stretch yourself toward what was previously unattainable. Without the right mindset keeping your confidence, self-belief and commitment rock solid, you are likely to become discouraged, which will lead to less practice and further discouragement until this vicious cycle causes you to drop out and deprive the world of your gift. The only preventative measure is to have the right mindset and I consider myself blessed to have glimpsed a world-class mindset early on in its rise to the top.

Alastair Cook recently became the first England Cricket Captain since 1985 to secure a series victory in India, during which he scored a staggering 562 runs in just seven innings. I had the chance to bowl at him back when he was a schoolboy. Even then he was a joy to watch, and he embodied everything you need to know about having the right mindset. He played with a smile on his face, dispatching ball after ball with joyful ruthlessness (remember the importance of fun). However, it was only when I enquired about him that I learnt the true extent of his mindset.

During his secondary school years at Bedford School, Cook realised he wasn't fit enough, so he joined the staff swimming club. This meant being up at 7am each morning, three times a week. His first cricket coach reveals that even on the mornings when there was no swimming club, 'He was in school by 7am looking for a net or a game of squash.' Jeremy Farrell, who was then Head of Cricket at Bedford confirms Cook's passion for improvement: 'He was a fantastic listener. He filtered information and advice and used it accordingly. He just about drove Derek Randall, our cricket professional, into the ground because he wanted to be on the bowling machine whenever he could, whether it was 9am or 8pm.'

To sum up the ideal mindset, three qualities stand out: find joy in practice, be passionately dedicated to discovering new ways to improve and have the discipline to persevere even when times are challenging.

Setting

Today Matthew Syed is one of the UK's leading sports writers, but not so long ago he was a world class Table Tennis player winning trophies on the international stage. His background tells us a great deal about the importance of setting. He grew up in the town of Reading, on Silverdale Road. In appearance, Silverdale Road is a street just like thousands of other streets in the UK. However, there is something very special about Silverdale Road, as Syed himself reveals: 'For a period in the 1980s this one street and the surrounding vicinity produced more outstanding table tennis players than the rest of the nation combined.' How is this possible? Two things conspired to make this tiny area a ping-pong hotbed. Firstly, a man named Peter Charters, who was the sports master at the local school. He had an absolute passion for table tennis and was one of the nation's top coaches, as well as being high up in the English Table Tennis Association. As a result, any of the children from the Silverdale Road area who attended the local school would come under the watchful eye of Mr Charters. Anyone who showed promise would be invited to hone their skills at the local club Charters had established, the Omega Club. This is the second contributing factor that made Silverdale Road so remarkable. The Omega Club was possibly the only 24hr table tennis club in the country. Each of its members had their own key and could use it to practice whenever they wished. This meant that Matthew and his contemporaries could spend blissful hours racking up the hours they needed to achieve expert status, all under the watchful eye of the nation's top coach. That is the power of setting. When looked at from this angle, the table tennis success of Silverdale Road seems like a logical progression rather than something truly out of the ordinary.

Clearly, setting is the soil from which the talent blooms. The same factors of setting that set Matthew Syed and his friends up for success were also present in the life of one of the world's most famous musical talents. Mozart is often held up as the epitome of a genius with a god-given talent. The truth is far more simple. Mozart's father was one of Europe's finest music tutors. By the time he reached his 6th birthday it is estimated that Mozart had already clocked up almost 3 500 hours of piano playing. Is it really any surprise he created what he did, given that he was able to call upon the instruction of one of the greatest musical minds of the time, who had ensured that by the time his son reached his teens he'd already had sufficient practice to be a truly world class performer? When one becomes aware of the setting into which Mozart was born, his ability can be appreciated as far more the result of human perspiration than divine inspiration.

The Talent Formula in Action

We can see the talent formula at work in the musical success of Ed Sheeran and the artistic achievements of Anna Mason. Sheeran, in one of his songs, claims to have done 'around about 1000 shows'. We know that in 2009 he played 312 gigs in a single year. He knew the hard work and practice that would be required and he had the mindset to go out and make it happen. Even at the age of sixteen he ensured he put himself in the best possible setting he could – being on tour with my friends and I, where night after night he was immersed in learning all about the art he was trying to master. He put in the necessary hours of quality practice, he developed the right mindset and he made sure he was in the right setting. His results speak for themselves.

Having read the above, you may have been wondering how Anna Mason could have produced prize winning art despite having not picked up a paintbrush in five years and having only just discovered the field of botanical art. It turns out she had been applying the talent formula from a young age. During our interview for this book, Anna showed me a photo taken when she was two years old, which shows her standing confidently at an easel with a paintbrush in hand.

Anna herself confirmed the extent of her practice and of the benefits of being in the right kind of setting: 'I look back to my childhood and I think that whatever the figure is, 10000 hours or so, I know that however many hours were required, I put them in when I was a kid. I loved to paint and draw and I was very lucky that my parents were always very supportive... with my dad in particular, I have some strong memories of holidays...I really remember, when I was six, him teaching me about perspective.' Anna was not only able to immerse herself in practice from a very young age – how many two year olds do you know who have an easel and a full set of paints? – but, crucially, she was also able to receive detailed feedback and instruction from her father, who was himself an accomplished artist.

Finding Your Sweet Spot

I am aware that whilst these examples may rewrite the myth that talent is something you are born with, they may perhaps reinforce the idea that there is a strong element of luck involved. You could certainly argue that the examples above were lucky in terms of their setting, with supportive parents, teachers or mentors present to help nurture and develop the talents that were emerging. Therefore, before we look a bit more deeply at how you can apply the talent formula, it might be useful to consider an example of how having an understanding of what inspires you, combined with an awareness of the areas where you have already undertaken significant practice, can help you find a sweet spot that allows you to give your gift in a highly rewarding way.

We find such an example in someone who is very dear to my heart, for she is in fact my mother. At the turn of the millennium, Prue Hardwick found herself at a bit of crossroads in life. She was soon to be divorced from my father and was faced with the prospect of having to rely on herself to earn a living for the first time in longer than she'd care to remember. Despite having recently completed an MBA, she knew for certain that she didn't wish to work for a company and be chained to a 9-5 office job.

Thankfully, Prue asked herself some very smart questions: 'What do I love doing?' and 'What am I already an expert at thanks to the number of practice hours I've accumulated?' Having begun her working life in the hotel industry, and then overseen a home business where twenty or more staff had to be fed every lunchtime, she knew the answer lay in the realms of catering and hospitality. She revealed to me how much she loved hosting guests and serving great food, but was very aware that she wasn't sufficiently practised to be able to cut it as a high-level chef.

The sweet spot Prue found was to set up a guest house. It allowed her to combine her love of hosting and her expertise in creating a great atmosphere, with her passion and skill for cookery. Starting small, her first establishment had just four guest rooms, but was such a success that within three years she had moved to bigger premises and had won the coveted 'Most Innovative Breakfast' award for our home county of Warwickshire.

My mother's example proves that it is never too late to discover new and rewarding ways to share your gift with the world. Whether you know it or not, your story has already provided you with the perfect setting and practice to do something you love. Perhaps not yet at a world class, Ed-Sheeran-type level, but certainly at a level where you can feel deeply fulfilled and be deservedly rewarded.

Masters and Disasters

Even when we discover the stories of people like my mother, it can be still be very tempting to think 'they've got something I haven't'. It can be equally easy to let that green eyed monster of envy raise its head. If ever you find this happening, help yourself by doing one very simple thing: get inspired. Each person mentioned above did not come from their mother's womb with any predetermined guarantee that they would excel as they have. They simply decided what they wanted and put in the necessary work to achieve it.

There is nothing special about them, certainly nothing that you don't possess. You know they didn't get lucky. You know they haven't got something that you don't...so don't get jealous, get inspired. Use their examples, and any others that work for you, as the definitive proof that anything is possible when you apply yourself.

And to help you even more, keep this saying close: 'Every master was once a disaster'. There was a time when Ed Sheeran couldn't strum a single chord, or when Alastair Cook couldn't even hold his bat properly, let alone hit the ball with it. Every master was once a disaster, and there are just three things that separate one from the other: Practice, Mindset and Setting.

The Importance of World Class

Each of the examples we encountered above is/was performing their gift at a world-class level. In the next chapter we'll look at how you can apply the talent formula and start taking the steps necessary to join them. Before we crack into that, it's worth taking a moment to understand the importance of attaining world-class levels of performance.

There are two prime motivations. The first is pretty basic and comes with a bitter pill to swallow. The world is not fair. If you want to reap good rewards from giving your gift, you cannot just be giving your gift at a good level. Whether actor, athlete, chef, poet or painter, there are hundreds of thousands of people trying to do what you are doing, and they wouldn't be doing it if they weren't good at it. And the vast majority of them, though they are good at what they do, are only reaping poor-average rewards.

YOUR PEAK POTENTIAL

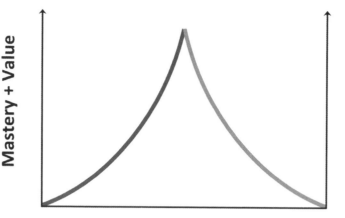

The Field of Your Domain

The above graphic shows what happens when you reach a world-class standard. You stand out from the field of your domain and, as a result of your increased mastery increasing the value of your gift, the opportunities and rewards that come to you will similarly increase. Clearly it's not enough just to be good. In fact, let's establish this as a mantra now: **Good is not good enough**. The vast majority of your field will be 'good'. If you want to reap good rewards from giving your gift, the bare minimum you have to be is excellent. To prove the validity of this hypothesis you need only look at the Olympics. Every single athlete who lines up for the 100m final is excellent, yet only one gets the fame and glory and vast rewards in the form of endorsements that come with topping the podium and taking home the gold. Without using Google, can you even name the athelte who came fifth in the 100m at the last Olympics? No doubt all eight athletes are bringing in enough to keep house and home together, but it is only when you step up to being truly outstanding in your field that you begin to reap excellent rewards. I understand that perhaps the bright lights and big pay cheques don't appeal, and that maybe that you'd prefer not to stand out and be outstanding. At least now you know that even if you only want 'enough', you're still going to have to be hitting consistent levels of excellence to be sufficiently rewarded. Good is not good enough.

World Class Service

The second motivation for striving toward a world-class level goes beyond personal. By aiming to perform at a world-class level, you are doing a great service to humanity. You are helping to set new standards that over time will become the norm for everyone, thus raising the collective standard of living. Thomas Edison was a world-class inventor and it is thanks to his persistence and dedication that you now take for granted the light bulbs in your house. Edison set a new standard that changed the lives of billions. Similarly over the course of a decade from 1980-90 Tim Berners-Lee and his colleagues set a new standard in how physicists around the world were able to communicate instantly with each other. Today you can access the internet from almost anywhere in the world via the smartphone in your pocket.

It may be that the domain within which you give your gift is smaller than that of light bulbs or the internet. Nevertheless, by striving for world-class levels of proficiency and by aiming to set new breakthrough standards as you give your gift, you have the chance to enrich the world and benefit lives in a way never seen before on Planet Earth.

So whether your motivation is personal – to reap at least good rewards – or you are inspired to enrich the lives of your fellow humans, it is essential that you are never satisfied with good. Instead you must make a firm commitment to master your craft to a world-class level. It is the process of mastery we will tackle next.

CHAPTER 6

Small Steps to Massive Change

It's Not an Overnight Thing

You know from the talent formula that practice time is an essential, unavoidable necessity when it comes to giving your gift to the highest standard possible. Therefore, it will probably come as no surprise to hear that, though your gift is of inestimable value to the world, the world is not going to change overnight as soon as you start giving it.

This is a very good thing. You know that as your talents and passions are grown, your purpose is created, clarified and honed. Therefore, whilst you have your long-term goals and aspirations as your guiding stars, you can be liberated through knowing you need only do what is right, right now. Typically, this will involve a combination of giving your gift as it is, learning from the experience and then using the lessons to improve your practice so that your levels of accomplishment increase, along with the value and impact of your gift.

If the last chapter presented the big picture on what is required to be giving your gift at a world-class level, this chapter focuses on the day to day details of what will be required. A good metaphor to keep in mind is that of driving a car in the dark. You might be travelling from Land's End to John o' Groats, or clear across America. You don't need to be able to see your ultimate destination. All that is required is to be sure you are on the right road and to successfully keep navigating the next 200m or so, illuminated by your headlights.

To bring this into the real world, Gandhi did not finish his university education knowing that 50 years later he'd be the catalyst for Indian independence. He hadn't even thought to concern himself with civil rights struggles at that early stage. His main worry then was how to successfully establish a legal practice, given that he was too shy to speak up in court. Even when he began fighting for the rights of indentured labourers in South Africa, his focus was simply on seeing justice done and on righting the wrongs that had been inflicted upon him and his countrymen.

Talents are grown and purposes are created. Gandhi spent 21 years in South Africa, more than enough time to have put in sufficient hours of deliberate practice in social activism to make him a world-changing force – especially considering he started almost as soon as he arrived by ensuring he was allowed to travel first class on the train despite having been thrown out of the carriage the previous day.

When you dive into living your purpose and giving your gift, the universe will support you. It is unlikely that Gandhi felt like his transfer to South Africa was a sign of success – more a last chance saloon after failing in his native land – but it was exactly what he needed so that he could become the man we revere today.

For Big Results, Start Small

If you can maintain the implicit trust that life will support you to achieve your desires, the question to answer is: What should you be doing to help life to support you? The answer is to know what your long-term goals are, and then to keep taking steps toward them. If you are an actor, perhaps one of your long-term goals might be to have a starring role in a production at the Globe or the RSC.

For now though, you are taking part in a small production in a local theatre. It is your duty to excel in this role to the best of your ability. The more you give your gift, the more you will realise that when you are doing what you love, everything you've ever done empowers you to do it.

To grasp how this might play out, let's look at the small local production again. Perhaps your role in the play requires you to speak your lines in a Welsh accent. If you invest the time and effort in truly mastering the Welsh accent, you will forever have a Welsh accent in your locker for any future audition/ role that may require it. Who knows, it could be that a good Welsh accent is one of the things the director is looking for when, years later, you audition for that starring role at the Globe you'd always dreamed of. If you put the work in now, you will reap the rewards indefinitely.

Establishing a Daily Practice

You may be surprised at the level of detail and dedication needed to ensure you can give your gift successfully. Perhaps you had heard the old myth that talent will always find a way. Bulls**t! Talent will only find a way if the owner of the talent never stops looking for ways to share that talent with a wider audience. Talent will only find a way if the owner of the talent doesn't just assume the talent will be enough, but instead practises and practises so the talent becomes outstanding.

If you are someone who had thought talent was enough, don't let it trouble you. You're certainly not alone. Now that you know differently, the first step is to establish a daily practice, to make a commitment to do one thing, even for just ten minutes a day, that will develop your talent and strengthen your gift. If this is something you've never done before then be prepared to be shocked at how hard it is to ensure you do it every day. Again, don't be hard on yourself if you miss a day; just make sure you continue your practice the following day.

Whilst a daily practice is not about results, you will be amazed by the results you see. In fact, my first published book of poems was the result of my daily practice. I knew I wanted to raise the standard of my poetry, so I committed to making sure that each day, before I did anything else, I wrote at least one poem. Six months later I realised I had enough to collect into a book. If I'd consciously tried to write a volume of poetry it would certainly have taken me longer than six months and the quality would almost certainly have been less good because I'd have been forcing it, instead of letting it flow.

One final thing to note about establishing your daily practice is the importance of making it something you will be able to do wherever you are. Even if I'd only had a napkin and had borrowed a pen, I'd have still been able to take a moment to write my daily poem. What will your daily practice be?

The Power of Habit

By establishing your daily practice, you will be establishing a good habit. I hope it will be the first of many, because the ability to create empowering habits is the single most important thing you can do to set yourself up for success. To commit to developing your gift to a world-class level is to commit to a process of mastery. We will discuss mastery in more detail later in the chapter, but I mention it now because it is important that you are clear that habits are what put the master in mastery.

I'm sure you've heard it said that we are creatures of habit. It surely follows, therefore, that if we create powerful habits, we will become powerful creatures. Examples from the footballing world certainly bear this out. By any stretch of the imagination Eric Cantona and Christiano Ronaldo are two of the finest, most influential players ever to have graced a Manchester United shirt. They had a habit that set them apart from their peers and set them up for greatness. Their habit was extra practice after the rest of the team had finished training. We know from the talent formula that their actions were helping to create a habit of footballing excellence, meaning they excelled on the football pitch as effortlessly as you or I might drive a car.

The example of Ronaldo allows us to see the power of habit at work. At the time of writing he is without equal when it comes to striking a deadly free kick. However, anyone who watched Ronaldo during his early days at Man Utd will remember a very different reality. Whilst everyone applauded his enthusiasm and bravado for stepping up and trying to shoot direct for goal from distances most players would never dream of, there was still a feeling it was a bit of a waste, since the ball nearly always ended up flying high, wide and handsome, deep into the back rows of the stands behind the goal.

Indeed, in the three years from his arrival in 2003 until the end of the 2005-6 season, he had scored only two free kicks. However, since 2007 he has scored five or more free kicks each season. Sir Alex Ferguson, his former manager at Manchester United, is under no illusions about what created such a shift in Ronaldo's free kick success rate: 'The boy practises every day, that's the reason he's so good. We go for a cup of tea and leave him to it. He practises all the time, 20 or 25 minutes after training, there he is with the balls.'

The Reach of Powerful Habits

Whilst Ronaldo's example shows how beneficial habits can be to the individual, the example of Eric Cantona shows the power of habits to have an impact way beyond the personal. In 2012 *The Daily Telegraph* ran an article describing how Eric Cantona 'transformed the landscape of English football'. The article documented how, from 1992 onwards, Man Utd set the standard for quality in the Premier League, and that it was Cantona who set the standards of quality at Man Utd:

> 'Before Cantona arrived at United, players trained in the morning and then went their separate ways in the afternoon.
>
> Yet the sight of Cantona practising his technique on the training pitch when the session had finished prompted his United team-mates to rethink their approach and join him for extra work.
>
> By the time United's golden generation of Giggs, Beckham, Scholes, Butt and the Nevilles came along, the Cantona approach was the accepted way of training at United, not an exception.
>
> Twenty years on, that professionalism is now a given in English football.'

This excerpt highlights the incredible impact you can have when you establish powerful habits. Cantona's habit of putting in the extra practice hours was so that he could improve himself as a player. However, his actions inspired his team-mates, and the success of the team inspired other teams, until the standard of the entire league was raised. This is a brilliant example of how seeking to set a world-class standard can provide a gift to the world...and it all starts with habits.

The Science of Creating New Habits

Of course, in simplest terms there would appear to be very little science behind creating a habit. Surely the more you do it, the more it becomes a habit? In essence this is true, but it is worth breaking down the steps that contribute to turning an activity into a habit. Luckily, to help you remember, the steps form a useful acronym: REPOH.

Step 1: Repetition

Not surprisingly, to begin establishing something as a habit you must do it repeatedly.

Step 2: Easy

The more you do something, the easier it will become. You will know you are on the way to creating a habit if the activity you are undertaking starts to become easier.

Step 3: Pleasure

The more you do something that then starts to become easy, the more you will take pleasure in doing it.

Step 4: Often

The more you are enjoying the activity, the more often you will want to do it.

Step 5: Habit

The more often you do something that is easy and which brings you pleasure, the stronger the habit will become.

If this all seems very obvious let's apply it to an example, so you can see how it could prove useful. Imagine you had to learn to write with your non-dominant hand. If you're anything like me, your first attempt would be painfully slow and the end result would look like a four year old's attempt at handwriting. However, the more you repeated your efforts, the easier it would become. As your efforts began to bear fruit, and the handwriting became easier, you would derive pleasure from your achievement (remember one of our human needs is the need for growth) in beginning to master something new. The more pleasurable you found the task, the more often you would do the task...and voila, you'd have created the habit of being able to write ambidextrously.

What is the relevance of this to you and your gift? As you develop your gift through deliberate practice, you will have to continually challenge yourself if you are to improve. With each new challenge attempted, you will begin by getting a lot wrong and not having as much fun as you might. However, now that you know what to look for, you will be able to see the first stirrings of a habit forming as you **repeat** the activity and what seemed impossible starts to become just difficult. By taking **pleasure** in the fact that the task has become minutely more **easy** you will be encouraged to do it more **often**...and you know what that leads to.

Being Persistently Consistent

The ultimate goal is to develop each habit to such an extent that you become unconsciously competent in executing it – like walking, where once you fell on your arse each time you tried, now you don't have to think about it; you just do it.

The key to developing this unconscious competence is consistency. In the section on establishing your daily practice, I stressed the need to be consistent. Everyone will miss a day, but make sure you don't miss two or three, because just like a muscle will waste away if it is not used, your habits will cease to be effortless and awesome for you if they are not reinforced consistently.

To help you build empowering habits and to allow you to effectively track the hours of deliberate practice that will be required if you are to develop world-class mastery of your gift, I've put together the 'Tiny to Tremendous' Mastery Masterplan in the Creative Uprising Playbook. I strongly recommend making it as much a part of your days and weeks as eating or sleeping.

The Curse of Expectations

The need to start small can present a challenging obstacle to be overcome, in the form of your own expectations. You may have heard it said that we over-estimate what we can achieve in a month and under-estimate what we can achieve in a year. Practically, what this means is that even if you are doing the right thing and consistently taking the necessary small steps, your progress might not match up with what you had expected. This may be especially true if the course of action you are taking is new, such as embarking upon some education designed to enhance your gift. If you do not see transformative instant progress, there is a temptation to be disappointed.

Don't worry if this is already a situation that has played out in your journey. We are brilliant at wanting to run before we can walk. Tell me this: have you ever committed to a new exercise regime, and hit the gym pumped up and motivated? Did you maybe overdo it a little, perhaps pulled something or overworked your muscles so that you struggled to walk for days afterwards. The prospect of then returning to the gym seemed far less appealing after that and the promised gym routine probably failed to bring forth the abs and gluets you dreamed of.

There is a profoundly simple way to remove the curse of expectation before it ever has a chance to trick you into thinking you're not progressing as you should be. Expectations are linked to goals, or to verifiable measures of progress. They are like a false inner GPS system that tries to tell you where you ought to be in relation to the goals it believes you ought to be achieving. If you want to remove the potentially fatal impact of unrealistic expectation, you must change the parameters of how you seek to progress.

The Mastery Key

The alternative to goal-oriented assessment of progress is mastery. In mastery the aim is not to achieve goals and markers, but rather to commit to the process of mastering the craft being studied. When pursuing goals, one's progress is quite staccato. A stop-start-stop-start procedure unfolds. One goal is reached, then the next is decided on, then acted upon until the goal is reached, whereupon the cycle starts again.

Mastery, however, is an unbroken continuum characterised by breakthroughs and plateaus. It is a never ending love affair between the practitioner and their practice. Along the way there will of course be trophies and awards. And certainly, your deliberate practice should involve small mastery goals that you work towards in your practice sessions. The key distinction to make is that these awards and goals are not the ends in themselves, just as oxygen is not the tree's end for photosynthesis. They are by products of the process. In simple terms: when you get the mastery right, the rewards will follow.

The sporting career of Craig Johnston is a great example of this. Johnston was one of the first ever Australians to play in English Football's top division. To get to England for a trial with Middlesborough his parents had to sell their house. However the trial didn't go as planned. Jack Charlton, the Boro manager told him, 'You might as well **** off back to Australia on the first plane because you'll never make a footballer in a million years.' Johnston was too scared to tell his parents what had happened and stayed in England, hiding out in the Middlesborough car park, earning a living by washing the players' cars and cleaning their boots.

When he wasn't washing cars or boots, Johnston was mastering his craft. He practised for six hours a day, seven days a week, deliberately practising the necessary movements and techniques over and over again for two and a half years. In an interview with *The Guardian* newspaper, Johnston revealed the kinds of challenges he set himself:

> 'I would put on a blindfold and sense the football with my feet as I dribbled. I put two small crosses on the wall and hit them with my left and then my right foot. If I was good and concentrated hard it would take me three hours. If I was poor, it would take me six hours.'

His work began to pay off and, when a new manager arrived, Johnston got his chance, becoming Middlesborough's youngest ever player at the age of seventeen and a half. An illustrious career with Liverpool followed, during which time he won a total of ten League and Cup Winners' medals.

Get the mastery right
and the rewards will follow.

Swinging Like a Tiger
(or 'How to get better by getting worse')

In the research papers I was given by Dr Ericsson, he expands on the nature of deliberate practice, revealing that it 'entails considerable, specific and sustained efforts to do something you can't do well – or even at all'.

The world of sport offers rich pickings from which to distil an example of deliberate practice in action, in particular the sport of golf, where a player's swing is one of the most analysed of any sporting activity. And there is one golf swing that is analysed more than any other: Tiger Woods' golf swing.

From 1997 to 2009 Woods won at least four tournaments a year and finished either first or second in the earnings rankings, except for two years: 1998 and 2004. In each of these years he managed only a single tournament victory and finished a lowly 4th in the rankings. The other commonality between the low-performing years is that they were both years when Woods was adjusting to a major revamp of his swing. Most golfers never change their swing except for the odd tweak here and there. At the time of writing, Woods has slashed and burned his swing three times, and is still adjusting to his latest change. A leading golf blog questioned the wisdom of this, suggesting that, 'Most rational golfers would not choose to overhaul their swing, to a different swing that they would have to completely overhaul again in 6 years.' From 1997-2009 that is exactly what Woods did. The other thing he did, in the two years immediately following each change - 1999-2000 and 2005-2006 - was to claim the majority of his 14 major championship victories (8 in total) and play a level of golf that had rarely, if ever, been seen before.

To put it all another way...he got worse, so he could get better.

Wood's journey provides a perfect microcosm to illuminate the mastery process. Mastery is a lifestyle. Its oxygen is deliberate practice. It wasn't that Wood's became a worse golfer overnight; rather he was paying the necessary price for progress. New habits take time to form, and while they are forming the body cannot perform at the consistent levels of excellence it once did. This is a point Woods himself was only too aware of when discussing his latest changes, admitting that it had 'taken a little while to build in new motor patterns...to develop the patterns and know what the fixes are.' However, as Tiger's subsequent victory-filled years prove, once the new patterns are laid down and the new habits are formed, it is possible to exceed the previous level at which you had been performing.

The diagram below offers a way to visualise the mastery process.

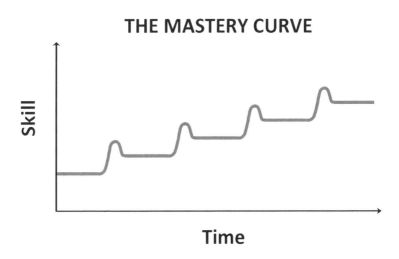

Adapted from the book "Mastery" by George Leonard.

You can see that, as you practise, you will have breakthroughs, where you will experience or glimpse a way of performing at a whole new level. In Tiger's case, this would have been when he perceived flaws that were preventing him taking his golf to a new level, that only a change of swing could overcome. After the breakthrough comes the fall, where you actually sink to a level below the breakthrough, as you attempt to bed in the new changes, incorporate them into the whole and become unconsciously competent in their execution. With practice, you will notice a slight improvement, but you will be nowhere near the breakthrough level you glimpsed. And you will stay at that level for what seems like an eternity. You are on the plateau. This was where Woods found himself during 1998 and 2004. He knew he had made the necessary changes to benefit his game, but time was still needed for the changes to become an unconscious habit.

As you know by now, there are no shortcuts in this process. It is just a case of REPOH, REPOH, REPOH, practice, practice, practice. Practice is the only cure to the plateau, and you should know that the plateau can certainly be a brutal, unrelenting place to be. This is why it is so important to ensure that you have fun in your practice and why you must find ways to fall in love with the process of practising. There will be times when you will seem to be getting nowhere – especially if you are undertaking deep deliberate practice, where making mistakes will be a necessary part of the mastery journey. In such times you need faith in yourself and in the mastery process, and you will definitely need to have fun and love what you are practising.

CHAPTER 7

Power Peers and the Power of Proximity

Part 1: Power Peers

Anti-social Monkeys

Now that you understand what is required to give your gift at world-class level, and practically how you can attain such heights, it's time to look at some of the resources available to you to make it happen. The single biggest resource you possess is your ability to choose. More specifically, your ability to choose your peers. We are not the products of our society; we are the products of our peer group. With this in mind, how can you be sure you are choosing your peers wisely?

To comprehend the importance of this, we need to spend a moment with some anti-social monkeys. Whether the following experiment took place exactly as follows is open for debate, but its conclusions are illuminating nevertheless. The story goes that a group of scientists wanted to test acquired behaviour in monkeys to see if any parallels could be found with human interaction. To do this they rigged up a mechanism in a cage, which would leave a banana at the top of a ladder freely available to any monkey that wanted to climb up and claim its prize. However, as soon as the most pioneering of the five monkeys in the cage reached the top of the ladder, the mechanism was rigged so that the remaining four monkeys in the cage would be sprayed with ice cold water.

Soon none of the monkeys in the cage wanted to go anywhere near the banana. The researchers then replaced one of the original, now fearful monkeys, with a fresh monkey who, of course, made a beeline for the banana atop the ladder. It had barely set foot on the ladder before the other monkeys had grabbed it and beaten it savagely.

Obviously you and your peers are not monkeys, but our primate friends can shed some disturbing light on what might be happening with you and your peers. The banana atop the ladder is your gift. Your peers are represented by the other monkeys. Although it would be very rare that your peer group were actually pulling you off the ladder and beating you for trying to give your gift to the world, sadly it is equally rare that your peer group would be really supporting you and pushing you up the ladder with shouts of encouragement. The reality is likely to lie somewhere in between the two.

The actions of your peers are not entirely their fault. As we learned in Chapter Two, we are at the cusp between two cultural paradigms. Consequently it is hard to find firm footing in today's world.

The Sufferings of Socialisation

When he was looking at what factors hindered people from experiencing the state of optimal contentment he called 'flow', Mihaly Csiksentmihalyi suggested negative socialisation had a significant role to play. The following quotation gets right to the heart of what he is driving at:

> 'A thoroughly socialised person is one who desires only the rewards that others around him have agreed he should long for…What matters is not what he has now, but what he might obtain if he does what others want him to do. Caught in the treadmill of social controls, that person keeps reaching for a prize that always dissolves in his hands.'

If this described the day-to-day experience of people in the Western world, there would surely be some stats to back up the theory. Sadly there are, and the weight of proof is overwhelming. In 2007 the UK came in last behind the US in a UNESCO report examining the well-being of children in developed nations, and in March 2012 the BBC reported that, despite a decline since the 1990s, suicide is still the UK's biggest killer of men under thirty-five. Add these stats to the fact that the number of convictions of young people carrying dangerous weaponry more than doubled between 1997 and 2006, and the picture appears pretty bleak.

We can parallel the impact of negative socialisation with the water that was sprayed on the monkeys. These stats represent the consequence of the damaging social norms we have allowed to poison our society, social norms that form the 'peer pressure' that influences the behaviour of your peers. Our culture has developed an addiction to negative news, a love of knocking people off their pedestal and glorying in their public disgracing, as well as a very warped sense of what quantifies success. If you're not a footballer earning hundreds of thousands of pounds a week, or you've not earned celebrity status either for getting your breasts out or for making a fool of yourself in the public eye, you're not fit to call yourself successful. Of course you could have worked hard and now be in a well-paid job that affords you a measure of comfort and security, but today that translates as being posh and out of touch with real people.

How is this relevant to you and your ability to give your gift? You are now armed with vital knowledge. You know the enemy, so to speak. You know what you and your peers are up against. If you choose to have as your peers people who are unaware of the impact of the culture we exist in, it is highly likely their interaction with you will be heavily influenced by the social norms of this dying culture. As you discovered at the start of the book, a new way is emerging. It is vital you understand that you and your gift have a key role to play in accelerating the arrival of the rising culture, and therefore it is essential that you surround yourself with inspirational peers who are riding the new wave rather than floundering in the wake of the old.

We came across the ideas of Jim Rohn in the opening chapter where we discussed the importance of having a powerful why. Mr Rohn was also very explicit on the importance of choosing you peers wisely. Pulling no punches, he suggests, 'You become the average of the five people you spend the most time with.' If you want to see how close to the truth this statement is, try this: add up the incomes of the five people you spend the most time with. Now take the average of those five incomes. Give or take a few grand either way, I'd be willing to bet that the figure you came up with is the same as your income. That's how powerful your peer group is. You become who you choose to spend time with, which is why you must be wise and aware when exercising your power of choice.

Choosing Your Power Peers

There are some simple tests to discern how truly empowering a person is for you.

1. Do affirmations and encouragement come out of their mouth more frequently than 'constructive criticism'?

2. Do you look forward to connecting with them, and do you leave their company feeling inspired and alive?

3. Do they challenge you in a way that may make you feel a little uncomfortable, but which you know is good for you?

4. Are they knowledgeable about the domain in which you are trying to give your gift?

If a person scores at least 3 'Yeses', they're likely to be one of your Power Peers, in that they empower you to give your gift even more brilliantly. A key distinction is that they should encourage you but also stretch you and challenge you to think beyond the box. If you want a little poetic tongue twister to affirm the point: 'Yes-men lessen the lessons you learn.'

You needn't think that if certain close friends do not score well in the Power Peer Test that you have to simply cut them out of your life; just be aware of the impact they might be having on your ability to give your gift. Perhaps make a conscious effort to enjoy social occasions with them without having to delve too deeply into other areas. You may well find that your friendship is actually strengthened because the negative influence they were having on your pursuit of your calling has been replaced by genuine enjoyment of spending social time with them.

Your Power Peer Mastermind

Your Power Peer Group will play two key roles for you and you for them: one will be as a sounding board and source for new ideas, the other being to hold you to account to ensure you successfully execute those ideas. To really get the most from the collective resource you are to each other, it is a wise idea to put a structure in place to ensure that as a peer group you get into the habit of empowering each other. One of the best ways to do this is to establish a monthly mastermind group.

Masterminding has been around for years, but with the explosion of the personal development industry it has begun to really gain popularity. Karl Pearsall is the founder of Masterminding.net and he has spent years identifying what makes a mastermind group successful. Karl reveals that masterminding is more than just gathering in a room and chewing the cud. It is a mindset, a skill set and a process.

When you gather with your mastermind group, you commit to creating a space dedicated to serving each other and honouring the following maxims:

- Collaboration is more productive

- Confidentiality creates trust

- Trust is an accelerator

- Team creates momentum

- Harmony synergises creativity

- Gratitude empowers

- Accountability overcomes blocks

- Momentum provides results

- Give more value to receive more value

Clearly, having a group of Power Peers committed to masterminding together is going to be a fantastic resource for you. Personally I cannot advocate Masterminding strongly enough. If ever you are feeling stuck or lost, a good Masterminding session will see you emerge reenergised, clarified and back in the game. However, if you feel it may be some time before you could formally establish such a group, you can do two things in the interim: 1. Know who your Power Peers are, and commit to spending as much time with them as you can. 2. GET AN ACCOUNTABILITY BUDDY! Seriously. Having someone you can check in with each week will see your productivity soar. If you have a list of ten important actions, an accountability buddy can be the difference between an 80-90% completion rate and a 40% completion rate.

Reaching for the Stars

If you could have a dream peer group, who would be in it? Perhaps if you were an actor you'd have Morgan Freeman and Steven Spielberg. Who are the stars in your domain? Imagine if you could have them in your peer group. In fact, right now, come up with three living people you'd have in your dream Power Peer Group. Got them? Great. Now, do two things. Write them a handwritten letter asking them for one piece of advice, or the answer to one question, then post the letter. When you return from the post office/box, get online and send them a message on LinkedIn telling them who you are, what you've done and why.

The fact is, when you're at the top of the tree it can be lonely. You'd be amazed how many people appreciate the effort of a handwritten letter and will be willing to reply in person. I suggest using LinkedIn because whilst the twitter and facebook accounts of most big shots are done by an assistant, often they will still personally check their LinkedIn account. If you don't receive an answer straight away, be polite but be persistent. Have you ever not replied to an email straight away because you were busy? So are they. It doesn't mean they don't want to reply, probably quite the opposite. At that moment, they simply have something pressing on their time, so be prepared to be patient, polite and persistent.

Here's another thing to consider. It is perfectly possible to have the leader in your field as one of your power peers without ever connecting with them personally. Remember, it's about who you choose to spend your time with. If you wished to up your game as an entrepreneur, it would be quite possible to immerse yourself for half an hour each day reading and researching the thoughts of Sir Richard Branson. If you took at least one thing a day from the research, pretty soon you'd be creating the same entrepreneurial habits as the Virgin founder, which would certainly not hinder your progress!

Part 2: The Power of Proximity

Dominating Your Domain

In order to sustain yourself and those who depend upon you by giving your gift, you're going to need two things: 1. Opportunities to give your gift. 2. Sufficient rewards from those opportunities so that you have 'enough'. To ensure these two things happen regularly you must be seen by your field to be of value to your domain. Your domain is the area of life in which you are giving your gift. The domain of judges, barristers and lawyers would be Law. For actors, directors, stage-managers and lighting technicians it would be Theatre. Your field is made up of the people who populate the domain, like the judges, barristers, lawyers, actors, directors and such in the previous example.

As we've established, you're reading this book because you have a desire to give your gift to the world and to be part of seeing a better world emerge. By doing this you are stepping into the role of servant leader – a leader who shows others the way by serving them. The place to really demonstrate your service leadership is within your domain, by adding value to the members of your field. Why? Because serving the field of your domain is one of the surest ways to ensure that in time you become one of the dominant players in your field. In his classic work on influence, Robert Cialdini identified what he termed the reciprocity rule. Put simply, it translates to 'If you do someone a favour, they will feel obligated to return the favour'. This means the more you can help your field to be successful, the more your field will be there to help you.

If you wanted to be really clever and exterminate two feathered flying animals with one rock-like projectile, you could serve your field and enhance your power peer group by setting up a masterminding group for your domain. It is likely that one or more such groups may already exist, but this should not discourage you. Far from it – the presence of other groups shows that the field of your domain values connecting in this way, and as the host of such a group instant visibility and credibility will be conferred on you.

Create Your Own Luck

If you want to start being known for your gift, first you must be seen within your domain. It's the key to making your own luck. If you want to be in the right place at the right time, be in the right place all the time so that when the right time comes you'll be there. It was a tactic that worked for a young bodybuilder trying to break into Hollywood. He heard there was a gym where casting directors would go to select the muscular guys they needed for their movies. Two weeks after starting to hang out in the gym, the young bodybuilder was offered a role in a film version of Hercules. Arnold Schwarzenegger never looked back.

Schwarzenegger had mastered the art of creating his own luck. Like the process of creating a habit there is a simple science behind creating luck. Luck is the synergy of two elements: preparation and opportunity. To be lucky you have to make sure you are prepared, so that when the opportunity presents itself you are ready to take it. Schwarzenegger had prepared – he had put the hours in at the gym so that he had a fantastic physique. He also made sure he was in the right place so that when he was presented with an opportunity he was able to seize it.

Your Net Worth Network

One of the massive additional benefits to serving the field of your domain is that you'll not only be creating your own luck, but you'll also be rapidly developing your network. If you've not already come across the saying, let me give it to you now: 'Your net worth = your network.' You already know it's all about relationships. What are you doing when serving your field? Developing relationships.

I mentioned it previously, but I want to go into a little more depth about ensuring you value yourself in a relationship. I have found out to my cost that by not being clear about the value I was bringing to a relationship early on, over time I began to be taken advantage of. Not through any conscious malevolent intent on the part of the other person, but simply because I had not clearly communicated the value of what I was bringing to the table. The result was resentment on my part and an unnecessary petering out of the relationship.

Parity is the keystone of great relationship building. If either party within the relationship feels inferior or superior then soon enough that imbalance will undermine the mutually beneficial harmony of the relationship. If you do start to notice an imbalance, the rule of thumb is to speak up early and clearly. If the person is not open to your comments and is not as motivated as you to return the relationship to an equal footing, then they are not someone on whom you need to be expending time and energy developing a relationship.

Trust and Expectation

Just as expectations can kill action, expectations can fatally derail a relationship. Your sole aim is to add value, add value, add value. You are investing in the relationship because you wish to see that person succeed. You trust that they wish the same for you and will do what they can to help you. However, if you let the blight of expectation creep into your head, the trust within the relationship will swiftly start to erode.

You are trusting that you are doing the right thing by investing your time and energy into the relationship. If you start to expect some kind of pay off, be it in the form of favours, introductions or joint ventures, then you will be poisoning the relationship. It is a challenge, but a challenge you must rise to: the challenge of being able to trust wholly and completely that whatever the payoff may be, it will be the perfect one at the perfect time.

Some worthwhile guidance is not to attempt to build too many relationships at once, but instead go for quality and depth. Once a strong bond is established, it will stay strong for years without needing the same time and effort as it took to establish it. This will free you up to keep making new connections safe in the knowledge you've a good deal of gratitude already in the bank. So go ahead and identify just three people in your field with whom you'd like to develop a fantastic relationship and spend the next six months to a year really making it happen.

CHAPTER 8

Get a Mentor

If, by this point in our journey, you trust me and reckon I'm trying to help, then whether you read this chapter or not, just do one thing: GET A MENTOR. Of all the investments you can make in yourself, finding a great mentor probably tops the list. Why is a mentor so vital? Let's take a moment to really delve into this question.

A mentor is someone who has been there and done it. Whilst your path is unique to you, there will be similarities in the challenges and obstacles to be overcome as you walk it. A mentor has the experience and expertise to guide your steps. They may not always be able to prevent you from falling, but their wisdom will make the fall much less brutal and they will be there to make sure you're back on your feet and have learned whatever lesson the fall was teaching you.

The Role of a Mentor

There are three stages to a mentoring relationship and at each stage the mentor's role will have a different focus. At first the mentor will have to do a lot for the protégé. At this stage the mentor will share with you their accumulated wisdom and show you how to do certain fundamental things that will be essential to your success. The comparison here might be to the father who is teaching his child to ride. At the first stage, the father is showing the child how to hold the handle bars, how to pedal, how to brake, and then watching as the child practises with the support of a set of training wheels. This stage can be summed up as 'Do everything, achieve lots.'

Next the mentor will be starting to take a less active role. The basics of the craft have been grasped, but at times the hands on nous of the mentor will still be required. The parallel here is to the stage in learning to ride where the training wheels have come off and the basic technique is solid, but the father may have to hold the bike and give it a little push so the child can get started. This stage can be summed up as 'Do less, achieve more.'

The final stage of the mentor's role is celebration. The protégé is now highly skilled in their own right, sometimes perhaps even more so than the mentor. The protégé may still seek out the mentor's advice and guidance, but it will be more in the spirit of collaboration and exploration rather than dependence. Here the child is now a skilled cyclist who enjoys going on bike rides with the father. The child may still ask the father which routes would be the most appropriate, but equally the child may take the father on a route of their own finding, to the delight of the father. This stage can be summed up as 'Do nothing, achieve everything.'

To give you a real life example of what this process might look like, let me introduce you to Luke Hartnett, a young rapper from my home-town who goes by the stage name of Trojan. I met Luke when he was fourteen. It was clear he had passion and potential, but lacked in the lyrical content, recording technique and performing mastery that would take him to the next level. At the time I had a very basic recording studio set up in the living room. Here my flatmate and I would spend hours with Luke honing his craft. This was very much the first stage of mentoring – my flatmate and I were doing lots and achieving lots.

During Luke's college years I began to play more of a guiding role. He was immersed in a music course at college where he was able to record regularly and work with like-minded peers on different projects. The hands-on instruction that characterised our earlier years was no longer needed, and was replaced by my input on how he could develop his voice as an artist and on the things he should be aware of when considering music as a career path.

Our mentoring relationship has now entered the third stage, where I spend most of the time celebrating his achievements and offering my advice only when he seeks it out. A high point certainly came in the summer of 2012, when he and his girlfriend gave an outstanding live performance at my wedding. Since then they have built their own recording studio and have set up their own internet media channel. It has been an honour to play a role in Luke's journey and I am profoundly grateful that it has allowed me to experience first-hand the incredible power of mentoring.

Coaching vs Mentoring

You may be thinking that the role of a mentor sounds to you a lot like the role of a coach. Certainly there are times when a mentor will be coaching you, and there are times when a coach will take on the role of a mentor, but there are certain subtle differences that are worth noting before we discuss coaching in greater detail.

A coach will do three things: 1. Help you be your best. 2. Help you reach your goals. 3. Help you to refine your process of mastery. You could rightly argue that a mentor might do all of these. You'd be right. The key difference is that a coach may not necessarily have the experience to offer certain key insights. A mentor has been there and done it. A coach may just have done a training course. That does not mean the coach's guidance and training will be inferior, but they may not be able to give the right experience-based wisdom when it is needed. Equally, a great mentor may not be a great coach. The best option then is to have both, and to understand what each bring to the table.

Functional vs Transformational

A coach will benefit you in a functional way. They will help you to improve in specific ways using tried and tested techniques. A mentor's influence will be transformational – they will broaden the scope of what you thought possible.

An example from the world of athletics highlights the point being made, and demonstrates the importance of having both in your corner. In 2007, sprinter Tyson Gay was the world champion at 100 and 200m. He thought he was running at the peak of what was possible. Then in 2008 some guy called Usain Bolt won the Olympics in a world record time of 9.69 seconds. Bolt's feat had a transformational impact on Gay, as he stated in an interview the following year: 'I look at track totally differently now after what Usain Bolt did last year…it's not about 9.7 any more you know, and it might not be about 9.6 any more, so I really appreciate him opening up that door for me to train my mind to run even faster than that.' After having his perception of what was possible transformed, Gay went away and worked with his coach (functionally) so that the performance of his body could align with what his mind now knew was possible. The work paid off too; just six months after giving the interview Gay became only the second man in history to run the 100m in under 9.7seconds.

This example shows the importance of having both a mentor to transform your perception of what you're capable of, and a coach who can help you make the functional improvements needed so that you can give your gift to the highest standard possible. Therefore, while I still stand by my conviction that this chapter's key message is GET A MENTOR, perhaps a caveat should be added – to get yourself a coach who can help you nurture the seeds of transformation planted by your mentor into fully realised results.

3 Ways To Get The Most From Your Mentor

1. Follow Through

Following through and acting upon the advice given by your mentor may seem like an absolute no-brainer, but, take it from me, your best intentions do not always result in action. Whilst there's no point stressing what's past, I'm aware that there have been a number of occasions when my mentor and I have shared similar conversations and I've received similar advice to that which I'd been given six months to a year previously. Having taken action at the second time of asking and seen how greatly I benefited, I frequently found myself asking, 'How much further along might I be if I'd taken action the first time?'

I don't want you to end up asking yourself such questions. I've found the single most effective way to ensure you follow through is to be invested in the relationship. It could be monetarily, or perhaps you will have to expend a lot of time and energy to earn the right to be mentored by your mentor. Either way, it is essential you have a stake in the relationship. If you have invested neither money nor time and energy into the mentoring relationship it is unlikely you will value it sufficiently to ensure consistent follow through.

If you are lucky enough to find yourself in a mentoring relationship that has not cost you either money or time and energy, then it may be that an alternative method of galvanising follow through is needed. In this instance, the drive must be internal, founded on dignity and self respect. If a starving person gave you some of their food, you would not disrespect them by not eating. So it is with your mentor. They are nourishing you with their wisdom. By not following through on their advice, you are refusing to eat the food they offer. By disrespecting them, you are disrespecting yourself in a grievous way.

2. Only Take What's Great

Whilst your mentors may be amazing, inspiring people, they are also just people. Unless your mentor happens to be the returning Jesus or a reincarnation of the Buddha, it is unlikely they will be perfect. Don't make the mistake at the start of the mentoring relationship of assuming they are perfect and raising them up on a dizzyingly high pedestal. When you discover they're just human, their fall from the pedestal you'd placed them on could be catastrophic for your relationship.

Instead, understand that they will not be great at some things and make a firm commitment only to model yourself on what they are great at. Remember, what you focus on expands and you become who you spend time with. So if, during the time you spend with your mentor, you focus solely on their flaws, the influence of those flaws will expand in both your mentoring relationship and in who you become.

In truth, the flaws of your mentor are also gifts, guiding you as to how you can be an even better servant leader. However, the real gold your mentor has for you is the greatness of their experience and expertise in the domain of your gift, so, yes, be aware of their flaws, but make sure you only take what's great.

3. Be a Mentor Yourself

This is really the glue that binds it all together, the step that will help you and your mentor to really optimise your relationship. If you are following through on their advice and are taking what's great, you are doing 80% of what is needed to get the most from your mentor. The final 20% comes when you become a mentor.

You may have heard the Taoist sounding phrase, 'The teacher is the pupil.' This is certainly the case here. By taking on a protégé of your own and developing a mentoring relationship from the other side of the fence, you will learn invaluable lessons that will help you take even more from any interaction with your mentor. Not only will you become smarter with the questions you ask your mentor, you will also be able to understand why they are advising you as they are. The result will be a marked increase in the trust and depth of your relationship, as well as a huge improvement and refinement in your ability to take what's great from the relationship.

Your Mentor: 'Setting' You Up For Success

In Chapter Four we learnt that 'setting' was one of the three pillars of The Talent Formula. It is more than worth noting that the presence of a mentor was a common factor in the examples we encountered: Ed Sheeran – Luke Concannon, Matthew Syed – Peter Charters, Alastair Cook – Graham Gooch, Mozart – his father. You know that deliberate practice *must* be the mainstay of your mastery efforts. To make the most of your practice, you *must* ensure that your setting affords you ample opportunity to seek expert feedback from your mentor/s.

CHAPTER 9

Being Outstandingly Resourceful

A Reality Check

If you are to successfully give your gift to the highest level possible, you will serve no one, least of all yourself, by being deluded about the challenge you are facing. The top ranks of any performance domain are fiercely competitive, be it sport, dance, writing, cooking or dog training. Indeed, it is this competition that is responsible more than anything else for the consistently improving standards we see in most creative domains. The domains of music and sport offer compelling evidence of this: what would have won you Olympic gold at the start of the 20th Century would now barely qualify you for the highest levels of school sports. For a band to be signed to a record label, it used to be enough that they wrote good songs and could play their instruments. Now they must have a following that can at least sell out a 1000 capacity venue before a record company will even take a look.

There is no point in wearing rose-tinted specs. Far better to be aware that only 1600 trainees are taken on each year by English football clubs. Of those, only 97 are still playing professional football (at any level) by the age of 21. Equally, there's no point denying that the country's top drama schools accept only 1% of those who apply, and even the less famous ones accept only 3-5% of applicants.

But knowledge is power. When you know what you are up against, you are certainly empowered because you know the standard you must reach. This is what gives drive and purpose to your journey of mastery. The above stats confirm what

Chapter Four revealed about the importance of honing your gift into a world-class offering. If you want to be giving your gift and being rewarded for it, there is one thing you simply have to be: OUTSTANDING. You have to be able to stand out and claim people's attention.

The 3 Cs of Standing Out

Standing out will take a lot of perspiration, a willingness to be vulnerable and share yourself with the world, and the courage to persevere even as it seems you are less significant and even more deluded than you ever could have imagined. However, if you can ensure the following three essentials are in place, you will be giving yourself the best possible chance of being a stand-out performer.

1. **Commitment**. Here you have permission to be foolish. The first step to standing out is making a commitment to stay the course until you get where you want to go or achieve what you set out to achieve. You may have to endure being regarded as foolish, persisting with your direction even when all the odds are stacked against you and all you're hearing is that only a fool would try to carry on. Success is found on the other side of failure. You must commit to going beyond failure if you want to stand out.

2. **Consistency**. Our old friend. Not only is it the vital ingredient in turning practice into mastery, consistency is also essential if you are to stand out. There are two things in particular you must be consistent with. Firstly, your message. As a servant leader, you must have a rallying call, a reason for people to pay attention to you and reward you for your gift. If you send out mixed messages, your audience will be confused and may

choose to buy into someone else whose message they can clearly grasp. Secondly, you must consistently share yourself with the world. It's no good having a consistent, inspiring message if you're not getting that message out into the world. In order for people to choose your gift, they have to know about your gift. You must be consistent in sharing yourself with the world.

3. **Creativity**. We will be connecting with creativity more deeply in a moment, regarding its importance in developing your resourcefulness. However, when it comes to standing out, creativity is a truly vital ingredient. Remember the science of creating your own luck? Luck = Preparation + Opportunity. If you want to get *lucky* and successfully stand out, you cannot do without creativity. Your commitment and consistency are your preparation. It is your creativity that will define whether or not an opportunity to stand out comes your way.

Standing Out Like a Quean

Let me provide a single example that encompasses all three elements, so you can see how the 3 Cs work together. In 2007 Laura Hamilton made a serious *Commitment.* She mortgaged her house and took a significant loan from her parents so that she could buy the lease on a small restaurant in Leamington Spa. In its first few years the restaurant, which she named Queans, didn't make huge amounts of money, but Laura had a supportive partner and her parents could see she was building something special.

As well as winning local industry awards for 'Best Restaurant' and 'Best Customer Service', Laura's *Consistency* and *Creativity* were winning her a growing army of loyal supporters, for whom Queans became the 'go-to' place for any special occasion. Laura was consistent in one area above all others. During the two years I managed the restaurant, I lost count of the number of times she told her staff and customers that her aim was for her diners to feel like they were having their own dinner party, where she did all the work and all they had to do was enjoy themselves. Laura measures her success by whether her customers feel relaxed enough to take their shoes off.

Considering Queans is a fine-dining restaurant, such a measure of success might seem counter-intuitive, but her customers love it. They love that here is a chef who is not concerned about Michelin Stars and plaudits, but who instead is passionate about giving her diners the finest ingredients, served in generous portions, in an atmosphere where they can be totally themselves, free of the need for any airs or graces.

The other thing that Laura's customers love is her creativity. The dessert menu is where she really lets it shine. While working at Queans I cannot remember an evening where I did not hear the word 'wow' at least once during the serving of desserts. Laura hand makes sixteen different flavours of ice cream, and as if that wasn't creative enough she then presents them on a menu that is a conversation piece in itself.

Laura has mastered the art of standing out. Her gift is a dining experience unlike any other. The world finally caught up with this fact soon after Matthew Norman, food critic to *The Daily Telegraph*, told a perplexed Laura she would need to install an additional telephone line. She understood what he meant when, a week later, his review appeared in the paper and he awarded Queans only his third ever maximum score. Both phone lines have been ringing ever since.

Being Seen in the Right Way

If you wish to use the internet to help you stand out (and I'm guessing you probably will in some way), it is important you realise the importance of online video. At the time of writing video accounts for over 50% of internet usage. By 2015 it is estimated that this figure will have risen to 90%. This means that if you want to use the web to help you stand out, you're going to have to be using video. Not surprisingly, there are no end of 'experts' popping up who claim to be able to help you get your message out there using video. Few, if any, of them have walked their talk like James Lavers, a former QVC programme director, who personally helped to create over £160m in sales for some of the world's biggest names in personal development, including Paul McKenna and Anthony Robbins. Lavers reveals that whilst there are innumerable tips and tricks you can pick up to make your videos more effective, there are three things that are an absolute must. Coincidentally, where above I provided you with the 3Cs of standing out, Lavers suggests there are 3Cs to creating an outstanding video:

1. **Character** 'Your Character is the most important thing. You've got to allow those quirky things to come through, especially if you are doing videos. People think being professional is being cold, distant and formal...actually that is the quickest route to no interest. Don't be afraid to be yourself...that means not being selfish and self-conscious, just letting it out.'

2. **Content** 'It is worth reading a bit about how to teach. I know this sounds bizarre...but when it comes to creating your content you can't just do stream of consciousness... you could be doing your viewers a disservice because it might not work with their learning style.'

3. **Complimentary** 'You've got to be able to give free

samples of your stuff. This is especially true for performers, creatives and artists. You can't just keep it all behind closed doors and keep on promising that you'll let somebody look at it if they give you money, or if they come to your event, or if, if, if. You've got to give them samples.'

Lastly, a few technical bits to put the icing on your great video cake: Have your camera landscape and at eye level. Speak slower than might seem comfortable. People who don't know you will find it much easier to take in what you're saying if you can speak at between half and three-quarters of your normal conversational speed. And finally…SMILE! This is really important. It lets the primal part of your viewer's brain know you are not a threat, and instead are someone they can like, trust and pay attention to.

Don't Take It For Granted

One final thing to note about standing out is that almost without exception, everyone can do it. With what you now know about video you can do it even more powerfully. Sadly, far too many people think they have nothing to share that will help them stand out. Perhaps you were tempted to believe that as you read this section on standing out. More often than not, the reason people may think like this is because they take their greatness for granted. The chances are you have something that already wows people, but because it comes so easily to you, you think nothing of it.

To help you uncover the stand-out brilliance that lies within you, I suggest you immerse yourself in the Stand-out Synergy System in the Creative Uprising Playbook. It will allow you to reveal your out-standing potential and then develop it into ways of sharing it with the world that help you really serve, share and stand out from the crowd.

Creating Your Own Reality

If the statistics of the reality check provided at the start of the chapter seemed discouraging, never be tempted to dwell on them. If, like Laura Hamilton, you can master the art of standing out with your gift, you will always find ways to make your mark and create the reality you wish to be living. An example from the world of music proves this point admirably, while serving as a fantastic bridge to the next part of the chapter, where we'll go deeper into how creativity and resourcefulness fuel each other.

You may or may not have heard of Sandi Thom. At some point your ears will almost certainly have heard her biggest hit *I wish I was a punk rocker (with flowers in my hair)*. While she has since faded from the mainstream limelight, back in 2006 she burst on to the scene with a unique bang. Thom seized on the opportunity presented by the fact that broadband internet speeds were now the norm by hosting '21 Nights from Tooting' – a series of twenty-one live gigs she held in the bedroom of her Tooting flat, which were then broadcast globally via the web. As thousands of people around the world began tuning in, the big record labels started paying attention and within three months she'd signed with Sony RCA and had scored a number 1 chart spot for her debut album and single – not a bad reality to have created.

Of course Thom didn't go from her bedroom to number 1 without the help of a dedicated team of management and supporters, but when you dive, the universe supports you. The bedroom broadcasts were Thom's idea and the universe supported her to execute them by ensuring that her previous years of hard work had attracted a strong team to her cause.

The Creativity Key

As Thom's example demonstrates, standing out is rarely a question of resources. It is almost always a question of resourcefulness. The more resourceful you can be in utilising the 3Cs of Standing Out, the more effectively you will stand out. When it comes to developing your resourcefulness there is no ability more essential than your ability to be creative. Sandi Thom created a buzz not because her music was the most incredible and original sound around, but because she found and incredible and original way to get people listening.

If you followed either the cartoon series or the big budget movies, you will know that Optimus Prime was regarded as the greatest Transformer. However, creativity certainly challenges his status, for it is creativity that *transforms* crisis into opportunity. Thom's challenging crisis was how to get her music heard out of the hundreds of thousands of others who were trying to get themselves heard at a time when the internet meant anyone who could pick up a guitar could call themselves a musician and start building an online fanbase. By thinking creatively about what could be done she discovered an opportunity to use the technology in a way that no one else had.

The Defining Problem with Creativity

One issue we must confront at this point is what could be termed 'the defining problem'. If you put ten people in a room and asked them to define creativity, the chances are you'd end up with ten different answers. However, they would most likely fall into one of two camps: practical creativity and imaginative creativity. Practical creativity suggests activity, using your hands to produce a tangible outcome – when you create a meal there should be something edible at the end of the process. Imaginative creativity is the ability to derive ingenious solutions and possibilities where previously a problem had existed. Often both types of creativity will be part of a single creative process, with the hands creating what the imagination had conceived.

Hereafter the word creativity will encompass the synergy of the two – assuming that you will take action on the potential your original thinking has developed.

Creativity: The Habit of a Mindset

It may already have happened. You may have started reading this section on the importance of creativity and before you knew it, your Creative Castrator had reared its ugly head and was whispering to you, 'Now you're in trouble....you're not creative. You never have any original ideas. You don't know how to be creative' and so on.

Absolute bull! Your Creative Castrator can go back to being banished; it couldn't be more wrong. I feel strongly about this for good reason. I believe one of the greatest fallacies inflicted on humanity is the idea that some people have the ability to be creative, whilst others are not that fortunate.

Creativity is a talent. And just like any other talent it can be developed and improved. And the best part? It's highly unlikely you'll need to notch up 10 000-15 000hrs of deliberate creativity practice, since the chances are you've already got a good few thousand hours under your belt. In fact, you most probably spent the first five years of your life being creative. Every time you played as a child, you were honing your talent for creativity. True, later on you may have let an education system or an office suppress that creative talent, but it's like riding a bike. You just have to get back on the bike. You may be a little rusty at first, but once you rediscover your rhythm and balance you'll be tearing up the road in no time.

To help, here's a couple of very simple exercises that will serve you whether you're a seasoned rider or you're just getting back on your creativity bike after a good while out of the saddle.

'The Creative Marriage' Exercise:

The strap line for this exercise is 'from something old to something new', hence the marriage part of the title. Tenuous I know, but there it is. The aim of this exercise is to think of two or more things that already exist and combine them in a way that makes something new. To give you a real-life example: my brother and I help to organise sports and games at one of the UK's leading music festivals. It's set beside an ancient Iron Age hill fort. To spice up the entertainment we created a game called Midnight Battle Frisbee. Don't worry...It's not as brutal as it sounds. We took a glow-in-the-dark Frisbee, 16 lengths of electric glow wire (that would usually be used to decorate vehicle interiors) and some glowsticks (usually a favourite fashion accessory of ravers and party goers), and used them to upgrade the traditional game of ultimate Frisbee so that it could be played in the dark, amongst the trees, in the epic setting of an Iron Age hill fort.

Let's try the Creative Marriage now. Don't forget that fun is creativity fuel, so allow yourself to have fun with this. When I tell you to look up, take the first two or three objects your eyes rest upon and then combine them into something new... look up!

'Reverse Brainstorm' Exercise:

This is a well known and very popular creativity exercise. No doubt the reasons for its renown and popularity are that it can be great fun and it can produce ingenious results.

It's designed to be used to stimulate innovative solutions to a creative challenge, such as 'How can we get more people to come to our show?' or 'What could I do to inspire more people more often.'

The Reverse Brainstorm begins like a traditional brainstorm, with the topic in the centre of a page and then you draw lines out to all the ideas you come up with...EXCEPT...in a reverse brainstorm, you must come up with as many ideas as you possibly can of how you can do the exact opposite of the desired outcome. If the topic being reverse brainstormed was 'How can we get more people to come to our show?' you would begin by brainstorming as many ideas as possible of ways to guarantee no one came to your show.

The next step is transformation, where you flip each of the ideas you've come up with. Perhaps two of the ideas you came up with in the first stage were 'Tell no one about the show' and 'Don't give people a good reason to come'. In the transforming stage, you might flip those to 'Find ways to tell as many people as possible about the show' and 'Give them a powerful incentive to attend.' Typically what you will find is that although you'd have thought of most of the answers using a traditional brainstorm, there are usually one or two absolute gold nugget ideas that you'd never have come up with using a traditional brainstorm. As always, let fun fuel this practice.

Switching on Your Creativity

Whilst exercises like the two above are fantastic tools, always bear in mind that the single biggest defining factor in your ability to be creative is your belief about how creative you are. If you believe you can be creative, you will be, and vice versa. There is a very simple truth underlying this fact, which we met in Chapter Two: 'what you focus on expands.' It would also be true to say that what you focus on, you experience. When you focus on something it occupies an increased presence in your awareness, dictating how you think and what you feel, and since like attracts like you will bring into your life more of what your focus is causing you to experience. What you focus on expands for the very simple reason that you are experiencing it. That is why your beliefs about whether you can be creative or not are so powerful. When you focus on 'I can't be creative', that is exactly what you will experience.

It is worth going a little deeper still, to look at the brain chemistry behind what happens when you say to yourself 'I can' or 'I can't'. This is one time it's worth being a little reductionist, since understanding what is taking place at the level of your neurology will allow you to see absolutely that your ability to be creative is in your control. I'm certainly no brain surgeon, so fear not. We'll keep it simple, but effective.

The diagrams below show a representation of two pairs of neurons. The first pair of neurons have just got the message 'I can be creative'. In response to this positive affirmation serotonin has been released, which has a huge benefit on overall brain function, allowing your brain cells to make more connections and therefore provide more responses to whatever stimuli they are given.

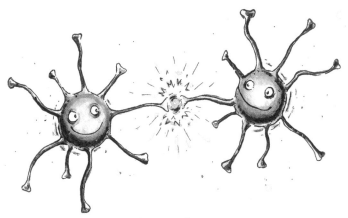

Are you creative? That's for you to decide.

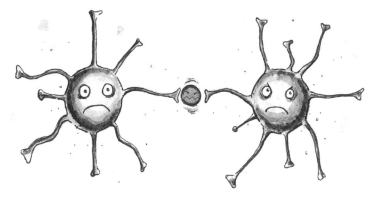

The second pair of neurons, however, have just received the message 'I can't be creative'. Consequently, cortisol has been released. Cortisol is the 'fight or flight' chemical. It inhibits wider brain function so that your body can focus on deciding whether to stay and fight or turn and flee. By saying you 'can't be creative', you're effectively telling your brain to shut down and run away because there's something scary that is threatening your well being.

What this very simple lesson in brain chemistry proves is that every time you affirm to yourself 'I am creative' you literally switch on your brain to make more synaptic connections and be more creative, whereas every time you think 'I'm not creative' you literally shut down your brain's ability to be creative. This is the 'how it works' stuff behind the truth that what you focus on expands through experience, so don't you dare ever again try to focus on the illusion that you're not creative. If you want to be, you are. Just keep practising.

Power Habits of the Super Resourceful

We'll encounter again the idea that what you focus on you experience in this section as we look at some of the habits common to resourceful people. Whether consciously or not, they know that what they focus on is what they experience and as a result are careful about where they put their attention.

There are three power habits common to resourceful people that consistently enable them to turn crisis into opportunity, and find a way to succeed when most would have given up long ago.

1. **Resourceful People Seek Synergy.** They understand the power of intention in creating the desired outcome. They know that if the intention is strong then the result can be something greater than the sum of its parts. 1+1 can = 3. To break this down, if you and I were to enter into a creative/business partnership, there would be the 1+1, which is you and me, however, there would also be the combination of what we each can offer that is more than what we each could do individually. Synergy creates a triple-win outcome: you benefit (win), I benefit (win) and the world benefits through our collaboration (win).

   In a real life context, this could play out as a band and a dance troupe wishing to collaborate. If they failed to seek synergy, the climax of the collaboration might be to go the traditional route and have the dancers dancing in a music video for the band, or something equally simple. However, if they were resourceful enough to seek synergy they might see the collaboration as the starting point for a musical theatre company. Can you see that from the point of view of the musicians and dancers, as soon as they were given the idea that they could be a musical theatre company they would be freed to imagine their artistic expression in a myriad of new ways that would exponentially expand the possibilities of what they could create? They each would benefit, and the world would benefit. That is the power of seeking synergy.

2. **Resourceful People Ask Better Questions** Here, you should be absolutely clear: adopting this habit will not just improve your resourcefulness; it will change your life dramatically. If you want a better experience, ask a better question. This works precisely because what we focus on we experience, and questions are one of the most powerful tools we have that help us to direct our focus.

Resourceful people have developed the habit of asking better questions. Instead of asking themselves 'Why can't I make this work?' or 'Why does everything always go wrong?' they ask more empowering questions, 'What would I need to make this work?' and 'Things appear to be going wrong...what might be the lesson I need to learn?' No doubt you've heard the saying 'Seek and ye shall find'. That's how your brain works. If you ask it a question, it will try to find the answer for you. Hence if you ask it why you can't do something or why something is going wrong, it will try to find answers to those questions. Therefore, make sure you're asking the questions that will lead you to the answers you need.

3. **Resourceful People Relish Challenges** The definition of a big game player is one who rises to the challenge when it matters most. Resourceful people have developed the habit of being at their best when it matters most because they have learned to relish each and every challenge. This means the bigger the challenge, the better they perform.

Being able to relish challenges depends on two things: how you perceive the challenge and how you manage the challenge. Perceiving the challenge relates to the importance you give to the outcome of the challenge. Your response to a challenge will be very different depending on whether you perceive it as a life or death situation or as just another item on your to-do list. Managing the challenge is knowing the factors that will allow you to be at your best when dealing with it. For example, if you are someone who does not respond well to pressure, part of your strategy for managing challenges will be to ensure that you develop a way of meeting challenges before time, money or any other pressure-exerting factor becomes too much of an issue.

In this context the perception and management of the challenge must go hand in hand. If pressure is something you don't respond well to, you're probably not going to do yourself any favours by perceiving a challenge as life or death, make or break. To do this would be to pile crippling pressure on you before you'd even begun. Conversely, however, you may be someone who is at their best when the pressure is on and you have to think on your feet. This doesn't mean you'd be best leaving everything to the last minute (unless this is genuinely what works for you); rather that you'd almost certainly benefit from breaking the challenge down and working through it in small chunks, each of which has a short deadline attached to it.

Whatever strategy of perception and management of the challenge works best for you, it is always worth keeping the following in mind: that resourceful people relish challenges because they know that each challenge will provide them with an opportunity to learn and grow. Or to put it another way: the challenge is the GOAL: Growth, Opportunity And Learning.

The Resources of the Resourceful

In addition to the three power habits, resourceful people are able to tap into three resourcefulness resources, which, when combined with the power habits, make them pretty unstoppable.

The Power of Meaning

Firstly, resourceful people make a conscious decision to choose the best possible meaning in any situation. We know that what you focus on is what you experience, so choosing to focus on an empowering meaning is a sure-fire way to ensure you feel empowered as your journey progresses.

You may have heard the hypothetical story of two brothers. Their father is a violent alcoholic who makes life a misery for the whole family. Thirty years later, with the father long since dead, one brother is highly successful and is a renowned philanthropist who gives to charities that support families dealing with domestic violence. The other brother is a penniless alcoholic and a constant burden on his family. When each brother was asked why they turned out as they had, both gave the same answer: 'My father was a violent alcoholic.'

What made the difference was the meaning each brother chose to take from what they experienced. Often it is the hardest circumstances that inspire the greatest actions. I hope you will take a great deal from this book and use it to make a difference to your life and the lives of others. However, even if you take very little else, I'd ask you to keep the following message close to your heart:

> *No Matter What Happens In Your Life…YOU Get To Choose The Meaning*

In fact, let's make it even more personal. Say it with me:

> *No Matter What Happens In **MY** Life…**I** Get To Choose The Meaning*

The Power of Gratitude

If you want to supercharge your ability to find a great meaning in whatever you create in life, then follow the example of all truly great servant leaders and bring the power of gratitude into your life. You may have heard it said 'gratitude is the greatest attitude', and I could not agree more whole-heartedly. When you are grateful you become great-full: full of greatness. Why? Because it is very hard to be grateful without lessening the influence of other less desirable qualities. It is hard to be grateful and remain selfish, since to be grateful is to give thanks for something, it is an act of giving. Equally, it is difficult for arrogance to exist where gratitude lives. To be grateful is to be glad and appreciative, whereas arrogance is characterised by contempt and disregard.

You could even go so far as to suggest that gratitude is the foundation of happiness. What you focus on expands through experience, which means that focusing on your gratitude for something will increase your capacity for gratitude to all things. You know from the lessons of Steve Jack in Chapter 2 that when you feel something, you attract more of it towards you. Thus, the more you feel grateful, the more opportunities you will be presented with to be grateful. And, of course, since we tend to be grateful for things that make us happy, it stands to reason that each new opportunity for gratitude must bring with it the cause of that gratitude: a reason to be happy. It's a virtuous cycle. The more grateful you are, the more reasons you will have to be happy. The happier you are, the more grateful you will be. You see where this is going!

In the spirit of gratitude I'd like to give you a gift to help you find gratitude if ever you are struggling to find it. The gift is a saying. The saying is this: 'Every moment is the most important moment of my life.' This may sound silly or trite, but it's true nonetheless. As a species, we currently interact with time in a linear fashion – we move from the past to the future through the present. What that means is that right now, you have never known more about yourself nor had a greater opportunity to direct the course of your future in the way you'd most like. If you wanted to, you could make a decision that would change the direction of your life and have an impact upon the lives of millions of people. That is why *this moment* is the most important of your life, and why '*every moment* is the most important of your life'. And this is why you always have a reason to be grateful. It is up to you to choose a brilliant meaning and be grateful for it.

The Power of Learning

The second you stop learning is the second you start dying. This is a belief that highly resourceful people live and breathe. When you can thrive while being squeezed and can embrace failure as being more valuable than success, because you know the great opportunity for learning they give, you will be well on the way to harnessing the potent resource that our ability to keep learning offers us. Like lifting weights in a gym or running shuttles improves your physical condition, learning keeps your brain functioning optimally.

These three resources reinforce each other superbly. One thing you can always keep learning is how to keep choosing a great meaning and finding reasons to be grateful. The more you can allow these three resources to fuel each other, the more your overall capacity to be resourceful will flourish, and with it your ability to give your gift in ever more brilliant ways.

PART 3
DELIVER

CHAPTER 10

Producing Revolutionary Opportunities

We Chose a Crap Meaning

This chapter will look at what it will take for you to be able to earn a living by sharing your gift with the world. Given that there certainly are a wealth of opportunities out there, you might be wondering why I titled this section 'we chose a crap meaning'. Well it has to do with the phrase 'earn a living.'

There's a real possibility we've got a lot of things backwards. Let's look at two hypothetical societies. Society A works only four hours a day and is profoundly happy. Society B work eight to ten hours a day and is profoundly unhappy. Which society would you consider to be more advanced? But which society sounds more like the one you currently live in? These are in fact real examples. Society B is our society, while Society A represents the indigenous cultures around the world that we have the temerity to dismiss as 'primitive' and 'backward'. I'm not suggesting you should return to wearing animal skins and living in caves (unless that's what would bring you joy). I simply introduce the alternative take on indigenous livelihoods as a way of challenging the notion that you have to 'earn a living'.

When you were born, you did not have to justify your existence by having a positive balance in your bank account at the end of the week. You were not expected to make yourself miserable just so you could keep from starving. However, by the time you hit somewhere between sixteen to twenty-five, you were 'on your own' and had to 'fend for yourself.' It has certainly not always been this way and it certainly is not like this in indigenous tribes, where the strength of the tribe is dependent on the tribe's ability to collectively care for its members.

Faced with such a perspective, it is difficult to ignore the possibility that 'we chose a crap meaning'. If we are the peak of evolution/God's creation, is the best meaning we can come up with to merely get by with what we believe is barely enough, plunging ourselves further into the mire of consumer debt, whilst 80% of the world's population lives on less than $10 a day? Is that the best meaning we can come up with? A world where just 3% of what the nations of the world spend on armaments would feed and educate every child on the planet, yet war, famine and ignorance continue unabated? If that's the best we can do, then we definitely chose a crap meaning.

Understanding Success

According to our advanced civilisation 'success' is synonymous with gain, excess and victory. If a business man/woman has made a lot of money they are successful. If a footballer wins a lot of trophies they are successful. If a person has more stuff than they need then many would think them successful.

Perhaps you are different. You know what 'enough' is, and that's a fantastic start. It is also worth looking at a far simpler yet much more powerful meaning of success. It was revealed to me by my wife, at a time when I was struggling. I was struggling because I did not feel successful (in the way our society defines it) and I was letting my feelings of failure damage my self–confidence and sense of self-worth.

As a performer, it would be dishonest of me not to admit that I take a thrill in being well received by an audience, especially if I have been able to serve that audience by inspiring them and enriching their lives in some small way. I realised as the penny dropped that if some form of fame and being well received, or cash in the bank, were the yardsticks I used to work out how much self-worth I allowed myself to feel, I'd always come up short. I'd only ever give myself the chance to feel 'good enough' for the briefest of moments. It became clear that the true test of success/achievement, one which we can all achieve in every moment, no matter what may be happening in the world, is to love ourselves and others wholly and completely and without judgement. Even if I found myself broke and homeless, and yet I was able to give love and to nurture myself and others, would that not be an awesome success? If I was booed at and laughed off stage, and yet was still thrilled to be alive, and could feel love and joy for the audience who had laughed and booed me, would that not be true success? Offer a child a choice between a priceless diamond and a bar of chocolate, and they will choose the chocolate nearly every time. More than anything else this proves we are not on this planet to acquire things that only have value because we happen to have collectively agreed they are valuable. We are on this planet to learn how to love each other courageously, truthfully and without compromise, and to celebrate that love with passion and creativity. Every moment you love yourself and others you are a success greater than any words could express. And what's more, you will find fulfilment effortlessly, because you will be content within yourself.

The Times They Are A-Changing

Thankfully, more and more people are starting to wake up to this simpler, more powerful definition of success. They are seeing stats like those presented earlier and are asking what they can do to improve things. As a result, the rising culture is gathering pace and it promises some fantastic opportunities for you to be able to give your gift. Two massive shifts are in the offing: how the world does business and how the world interacts with money. Both are in the process of being completely revolutionised.

When it comes to our relationship with money, one of the servant leaders pushing the envelope of change is Simon Dixon, who is the founder of BankToTheFuture.com and one of the UK's leading proponents of banking reform. Simon reveals that one of the key characteristics of this change will be 'a shift from traditional methodologies of measuring one's ability to be credit worthy or to lend or to raise finance, to one where your ability to reach out and the size of your voice is actually influencing your ability to access capital in the future.' In layman's terms, this means that your ability to access money will no longer depend so much upon your credit rating, or even whether you have a bank account, but on the amount of social capital you have created.

Social capital is becoming an increasingly popular, yet misunderstood idea. According to Dixon, social capital 'is not how many likes you have on facebook or how many followers you have on twitter, though that's a part of it. Social capital is the relationships you have…what it is measured by is, when you're posting on facebook, how many people are actually engaging with your content and with what you're saying. Social capital is how many people one can influence both online and offline.'

The rise of crowd funding platforms and the burgeoning growth in the use of social capital is fantastic news for you, someone who seeks to inspire by sharing their gift with the world. The more you inspire others, the more your social capital will soar. And here's the better news: even in traditional money terms the signs are very favourable for you. According to Polly A. Bauer, who is an online retail expert and one of the founders of the credit card industry, online retail is expected to grow at between 15-20% a year. By 2016 it will be a £400 billion market. That's a pretty massive pie. In fact, you need to inspire less than a thousandth of one percent of it into investing in your gift and you'll be doing handsomely for yourself – especially if you put into practice what I'll be sharing with you in the rest of this chapter.

It is not just the explosion of online business that is set to benefit you. The vast amount of information at our fingertips, thanks to the web, has resulted in a profound search for meaning. Just look in the window of any bookshop and you'll see no end of self-help and personal development books offering everything from goal setting to quantum healing, via urine therapy and spiritual marketing. This points to one incontrovertible fact: more than ever before, **people are seeking inspiration**. They feel something's not quite right and they're looking for answers.

When you give your gift courageously and with the intention to serve, you will inspire. Fact. Therefore you have what people want. Now it is a case of finding which people in particular want what you're offering and giving it to them.

The Entrepreneur Revolution

Luckily for you there have never been more ways for you to find who wants what you have, build a relationship with them and give them your gift in a mutually rewarding way. Right now there is what can only be described as a sea change sweeping the globe and changing the face of business. To describe what is happening Daniel Priestley, bestselling author of *Become A Key Person of Influence,* coined the term 'The Entrepreneur Revolution'. He suggests we are entering, 'a new era where, rather than large corporations that try and dehumanise the process...we're now seeing that small, entrepreneurial teams are the value creators in the economy.' At the heart of this transfer of power is technology, in particular smart phones and the web, which allows small businesses to shift from merely being players in a local market, to being genuine competitors on a global scale.

Priestley defines these companies that are emerging as Global Small Businesses, because of the way they are taking advantage of the fact that today you can connect with customers around the world and can run your entire business wherever you are from the phone in your pocket. You can have your graphic designer in Switzerland, your factory liaison in China, your distribution hub in India and your admin team in Liechtenstein. You can coordinate all of this, manage projects, share data and allocate resources using apps specifically designed for the task. You can even work on your home computer via your phone or tablet from almost anywhere in the world.

It has never been cheaper or easier to start a business, and the tools and resources available to budding entrepreneurs mean the playing field is rapidly being levelled. Today a big firm like L'Oreal is no longer the go-to authority in their field. Instead of looking for L'Oreal make-up tips and heading to the company's website, women (or men) are more likely to search on YouTube for the relevant video, which could be provided by a teenage girl using her phone's camera and the mirror in her bedroom. Big firms with a long history can no longer rely on their status and reputation to bring them business. They are no longer fighting with other big businesses to decide the best way to carve up the pie. In fact their pic-nic is being ruined by what Priestley terms 'global small business ants', who are ignoring what the big businesses are doing and instead are working with all the other ants to ensure that as many as possible get enough of the pie to sustain them.

A whole new breed of creative entrepreneur

This shift in the power dynamic of business is not just a fad or temporary phenomenon; it is wholesale and will only become more pronounced in its prevalence and influence as the twenty-first century unfolds. Of course this is great news if you're a small business owner, or someone who wishes to be in business, but what about you? How might these sweeping changes enhance your ability to give your gift and be rewarded for doing so?

The Art at the Heart of the Entrepreneur Revolution

Priestley suggests it is a great time to be a performer or in the creative arts. During our interview, he summed up the reasons why he believes this so well that I'm just going to let you appreciate his words.

> 'A couple of hundred years ago humans were defined by our ability to move objects with our hands. The

most valuable people were those who were good with a sword, with a bow, or even artists – painters, sculptors, architects. Then we created machines that were better at using hands than humans were. We created sewing machines, which were better than tailors. We made hands redundant, so suddenly people who were good with their hands were no longer very valuable in the economy.

The next stage was people who were good with their heads. The industrial revolution was all about strategic thinking. It was about logic and reasoning, crunching the numbers, widening the margins. Over the last 10-15 years, we've created machines that can out-think us. They're called computers and their strategic thinking is now making great thinkers redundant.

So that makes us ask the question: where do humans have any competitive advantage? If we're no good with our hands and no good with our heads, the only thing left is actually our passion and our heart, the networks we have and the enthusiasm we can bring to a project, our creativity, our innovation.'

'Passion', 'heart', 'creativity', 'innovation': these are qualities and talents that a creative individual like you already has in abundance. Therefore you are perfectly poised to ride this new wave that is breaking, a wave that is the synergy of the rise of social capital and the Entrepreneur Revolution, underpinned by the flowering of the rising culture.

Indeed, Priestley concurs with Simon Dixon that performers and artists have a huge role to play in the coming years because the ability to inspire people to engage is becoming so crucial: 'People have to care…companies are more interested in creating an engaged audience of 100 000, than broadcasting to 1 million people watching TV who don't care...We're looking for genuine, real artists to do stuff that people care about.'

All of this points to a Creative Uprising to accompany the Entrepreneur Revolution. As money and business changes, becoming more caring, more personal and more far-reaching, there will be a surge in the need for artistic talent, creativity and performance that can capture people's attention, genuinely engage them and inspire them to care. The world needs your creativity. It needs you to be a leader. Not just a servant leader, but a creative leader – one who will choose wisely how you give your gift to the world, so that the fruits of your creative performance will help others to enrich the world. To be such a leader, you must be able to share your gift and be rewarded for doing so. It's not good leading if a lack of money means you cannot feed yourself.

The Two Choices

No matter what you might think about money, the human species has not yet learnt to do without it in some form, so you're going to have to bring in some cash somehow.

According to Priestley you have two choices. One is to embrace being a struggling artist and accept that you'll need a second job, a benefactor or a rich partner in order to pay the bills. For some this is the only choice they feel is viable. They live for the sake of their art. If that is you, great, but don't expect the money to come. Instead, acknowledge your choice and embrace the 'struggling artist' lifestyle. The other choice is to be clear that you do want to make a living from your gift. If this is you, then you must accept that you will have to be part artist, part entrepreneur, at least for as long as it takes for you to attract the right team around you, but even then you will still have to have significant input to ensure your gift is keeping food on the table.

If you choose to go down the struggling route and get a day job to cover the bills, bear in mind the importance of trying to find work in an area that will enhance some aspect of your gift. I developed the ability to put my poetry to music when I was being paid to do youth work based around teaching young people how to write rap lyrics. During the sessions, I helped young people to improve their writing skills, and they improved their own rapping skills by teaching me how to rap. If you can be paid for a valuable service that is also helping you to improve your gift, you will be seriously harnessing the power of synergy.

If you would prefer the path of the not-so-struggling Artist/Entrepreneur, then it is important to know what you'll need to do to make this choice work for you. To help you get clear on this immediately, I ended the interview with Daniel Priestley, who is a very successful and respected entrepreneur, by asking for the three top tips he would give to people like you who choose the path of being entrepreneurial and seeking to earn a living from their gift. His responses were brutally honest, but, I hope you'll agree, all the more useful as a result.

Top Tip 1: Accept that it's going to be hard and that it never ends

'There is a big difference between the person who's imaginative and the person who's creative. Creativity requires blood, sweat and tears. It requires risk, it requires late nights, long time frames and it requires a commitment to bring something into the world that is whole and complete...Expect the journey to be rough and just remind yourself that this is the greatest time in history, to be born in a first world country and the thing that you consider to be hard is turning your passion and your art into money.'

Top Tip 2: Learn to sell and pitch

'You can only do the work after you've won the work. In fairy land, we all want to turn up and just do the work... The commercial reality is that if you want to be successful with anything you have to win the work and then do the work, so you've got to learn how to sell, how to pitch and how to put together a deal.'

Top Tip 3: Build an Empire

'Understand that you're going to need to create a number of products and services around your art...You've got to look for multiple angles you can monetise. You've got to build several products, several services that clip together to form a business... It's never ever one thing, it's always an empire you've got to build around what you do.'

If you're already trying to embrace the entrepreneurial side of sharing your gift with the world, these three tips may not be new. Certainly, from what we have learnt about mastery and practice, you know that it is going to be hard and it never ends. It is also all the more rewarding for this very reason. In this context, it is certainly worth reiterating what Priestley says about perspective. Though it may be tough and hard work bringing your gift into the world in a way that enriches others and sees you rewarded, it is essential never to lose sight of the fact that the challenge you are facing is not having to dig ditches, endure famine or fetch water from miles away. You are embracing the challenge of turning your gift into a way of sustaining your self. That's a pretty great first world problem to have, and one of the best ways you can start to make it happen is to create great products around your gift.

Products...but I'm an Artist!

Get over it! Mastering the talents of your gift is completely and utterly essential, but it's only 20% of the battle. The other 80% is getting your gift out there and being rewarded for it.

Sadly, in the creative world, the stereotype of the struggling artist tends to prevail. One consequence of this is the common perception that seeking to earn money and being conversant with the language of business will somehow poison what is being created. It is not uncommon to come across people who take offence if you start talking about how you're trying to 'bring a product to market'. They accuse you of jumping on some planet raping corporate bandwagon, before running off and fornicating with a tree.

How do I know this is true? I used to be one of them. I even once earned the nick-name 'Angry George' because all my poetry consisted of at the time was angry, ranting diatribes against anyone who had the temerity to wash and earn some money.

Look, I still love spending time with nature. I've even been known to hug the odd tree from time to time...but I can't help but be amused when I look back on the perspectives I used to have.

The simple truth is that almost every living thing is a producer in one way or another. The apple is the product of the apple tree. Milk is the product of the cow. There is no need to feel uncomfortable with the word product, or to think that it would in someway be wrong for you to create products that help get your gift out into the world. The danger comes when those who benefit from the milk or the apple cease to see the tree or cow as living entities worthy of being treated with dignity and respect. To see the cow or tree as nothing but numbers on a spread sheet, whose sole reason for existing is to swell the figures in the profit column is to create a damaging rift in the web of life that connects all things.

The truth is you are blessed to be able to use your imagination to conceive and create a multitude of products/offerings that can help you share your gift, enrich the world and ensure you are justly rewarded. However, if you think of the products you create as nothing but ways to make money, if they have no value to you beyond what you are choosing to charge for them, then they will become joyless and lifeless and uninspiring, which is the very antithesis of what you need them to be. So take joy in creating and distributing your products, celebrating the fact that they are how the world can experience your gift.

The Asset is You

Your products may show up in many forms. This book is one of my products. Among other things I also have audiobooks, poetry gifts, workshops and talks. Each of your products will be created from the assets you have, which combined together comprise your gift. If we were to attempt to sum up your assets in another way, we could say that your assets are the fruits of your mastery – the expertise you have acquired and the helpful lessons you may have learned. Not surprisingly, one of the best ways to generate an income stream is to teach others what you know. What's also pretty cool is that it turns out that one of the best ways to really make sure you've mastered something is to teach it to others. Now that's what I call a triple win – you are rewarded (win) for helping someone else (win) in a way that helps you (win).

This is also where the internet really comes into its own. By setting up your own online courses you can be teaching and nurturing a community of people without ever needing to sit with them in a physical classroom or having to shoulder the expense of a venue in which to deliver your training. This is a field that James Lavers has led the way in since giving up his TV work. He designed a system he called The Lazy Coach Way, which was an online course he created to teach others how to…create an online course!

In our interview, he was quick to stress two things. One is that you almost certainly have something to teach. If you have a skill that others would like, then you have something to teach, so don't be selfish and hide it from the world. The second thing is that you must find out where people who would want your gift hang out online and make friends. Lavers confirms the importance of serving and engaging with the field of your domain: 'One of the most important things you can do, is to connect first. Too many people try to do the commerce side first and I'd say connect first. I think a greatly under-rated quality is being nice. Be nice to people so that you get a name not only for what you do, but also for your character.'

You will find that creating an online course can help to create fantastic synergy for you. Not only is it a brilliant way of helping others and sharing your gift with them, it is also a high value product that can really wow. Because of this, it is certainly worth investing in the education that will help you to ensure your teaching really delivers. To get you started, you'll want to check out the Create My Curriculum section of the Creative Uprising Playbook.

Climbing the Product Pyramid

Of course, teaching what you know is just one way to create a product from your gift. However, even before you decide on the products you wish to create, it may be wise to have a structure and system to fit them into. Not only will this help you to be clearer on the kind of experience you want your supporters to have, it will also enable you to know what your price points should be and what you'll need to have in place to ensure each product is a success.

I've come across the following structure in many places, so I make no bones about putting a different name on something that already exists. Daniel Priestley calls it the 'Ascending Transaction Model'. I've also heard it called a 'product staircase' or 'the funnel'. For our purposes, I'd like to introduce you to (cue drumroll):

To ensure you never forget that the success of your products and the impact of your gift depends on the quality of the relationships you forge, I have chosen to present The Product Pyramid in the language of intimate relationships.

Each level of the pyramid represents steps your supporters can take on the journey of discovering you. I choose my words very carefully here. Be clear that you are aiming to attract supporters not customers. You are aiming to build a tribe who will relish discovering you and supporting you. How they discover you will be through the products and services you offer. Remember, even if you think you are too artistic to be associated with words like products and services, that's exactly what you are offering your supporters. The painters' products are their paintings. Their services are their commissions and exhibitions. Use different language if you prefer, but be clear on the reality of the situation.

As your supporters progress up the pyramid, two things increase: the amount they will be rewarding you for the value you are adding (aka price) and the amount of face to face time they get with you. The thing you can never get back once given is your time. Time is not money. Time is your life. Therefore it's right that those who have invested more in supporting you to give your gift to the world should get more direct access to you.

Courting Products

At the first step of The Product Pyramid you are **Courting** your potential supporter. If you wanted to woo someone, you might bring them chocolates or send them flowers – you would give them gifts. The products of the Courting stage are free gifts designed to begin the transformation of a curious person into your supporter. You cannot avoid this step. People now expect to be given something for free before they buy. Musicians will nearly always have a free track you can download when you visit their site. Actors might have their showreel on their site, or a link to watch them in a short film. Anything can serve as a gift as long as it is enriching the experience of the person receiving it. Your gifts (it's a good idea to have a number) must add value to your potential supporters, which is why knowing what they want and the kinds of people they are is so essential. We will cover getting to know your supporters' needs in the next chapter.

Once people have appreciated your gifts and received value from them, they will be ready to invest in supporting you. I use the word invest because if they are choosing to part with their hard-earned cash, they will certainly be expecting a return from you. If you are a musician, they may be ready to buy your album, trusting that the pleasure they will receive from listening to it will be more than worth the £10/$15 it costs. Once a supporter is ready to pay for your product/s they move on to the next stage of the product pyramid.

Dating Products

When you move from Courting to Dating, you will need to step up the level of value you are adding. As stated, it is about ensuring the supporter receives a return on their investment. If someone is willing to invest time, energy and money in connecting with you it is because they have a need, or needs, they believe you can fulfil. Therefore the products within your Dating level must do three things if both parties are to enjoy the Dating experience.

1. They have to demonstrate how awesome your gift is. When you're on a date, you hope the person you're with will be sufficiently impressed to want to date you again. Therefore your Dating products should wow the supporter, whilst showing them you have a profound and vital gift, which you are outstanding at giving.

2. A Dating product should allow you to discover a bit more about the person you are dating. On a date you will naturally ask questions about favourite movies, brothers and sisters etc. In the product context, a Dating product should require the potential supporter to share something about themselves – most often an email address so you can stay in touch, but ideally a facebook like and twitter follow too.

3. A Dating product should leave the potential supporter feeling great and wanting to take things further. Is this not what the perfect date should do? You both leave feeling like you're walking on air and you can't wait till the next time you connect. To leave them feeling great your Dating product should enrich their life in some way, but not so much that they have no need to take things further with you.

Mating Products

Once you have shared a few dates, there may come the magical moment when you go back to one of your residences for 'coffee'. Welcome to the **Mating** stage. At this point your supporter needs to be satisfied. They are inviting you to get to know them on a deeper level and you should reward their trust with instant gratification. If being a musician was part of your gift, once your supporter is ready to move from the Dating of buying CDs and T-shirts, you might offer a Mating product such as the chance to spend a day with you at your studio, where you'll give them some tips and tricks on how they can get the best out of their recording and song-writing. The key thing to remember about a Mating product is that because its price will be much greater than at the Dating stage, you must be able to deliver massive value without it taking up too much of your time and effort, which must be reserved for the latter stages of the pyramid and for any other ways you see fit to share your gift. This is why one day, but with lots of face to face time, works well. The supporter gets to be up close and personal with you (very high value), but only for a short period (one day).

Relationship Products

If your Mating product/s are appreciated, your supporter may be ready to move to the **Relationship** stage of your product pyramid. This is where, thanks to the groundwork laid by your Dating products, the supporter feels that you are the best person to meet the needs they have: that it is your gift above all others that, right now, will make their life better.

To have their needs met and to experience your gift fully, your supporters will be willing to make a significant investment, and you should be happy to let them. Your Relationship product will require a significant commitment of your time – aka your life – therefore it is right that your supporter be invested in it to such an extent that they are motivated to follow through on what you share.

When you get to the Relationship stage your job is to wow your supporter by under-promising and over-delivering. You must leave them marvelling at how lucky they are to have discovered you. You have to meet your supporter's needs in such a complete way that they will speak about you to all their friends in the most glowing terms. Returning to the musician example, the supporter may have loved the Mating experience and now wants to learn even more from you, so your Relationship product might be a six-week online course that offers a masterclass in guitar playing and song-writing. Remembering that you must under-promise and over-deliver, you might include as unannounced bonuses a weekly question and answer session and a series of videos on how to record high-quality songs in your bedroom.

Living Together Products

If the Relationship proves rewarding for both sides, the next step would be **Living Together**. In the product context this would be an enhanced version of your Relationship product. Since the investment required and the demands on your time would be even higher, you might decide to make it an exclusive product, only available to supporters who meet certain qualifying criteria, one of which should be the ability to pay a premium price. Continuing with the musician example: after the online course of your Relationship product, your Living Together product might be a musical mastermind group, where once a month you would gather with a small group of your supporters (up to 20) to share with them everything you'd learnt about how to make it as a successful musician and you set up the group in such a way that the members become Power Peers for each other and accelerate each others' successes.

Engagement Products

The penultimate step on The Product Pyramid is **Engagement**. As implied, there is a commitment from you at this stage. At this stage you are aware how much value supporters who reach this stage are adding to your life and to your ability to share your gift with the world. Consequently, you must commit to ensuring you add equivalent value to their lives. In the musician example, you could, after successfully impressing your mastermind group, invite the supporters who had completed it to step up to an even more exclusive Engagement mentoring service, where you work with a maximum of five supporters and make their needs your needs. This means you would be as committed to their success as they are. You would share your contacts in the music business, open doors for them to perform and expose them to your supporters. You would be giving them the value of all the relationships you had spent a lot of time, energy and money to develop. Not surprisingly, their required investment would be at a significant level, but the value you would be offering would far exceed any amount of money they could pay. Again, you would almost certainly want some criteria in place, since you would want to be sure that whoever you accepted into your Engagement level product was in a position to be able to make the most of it. You would effectively be aiming to set them up for life. You would want to be sure that they were capable of and committed to getting the best from working with you.

Marriage Products

Finally there are the products you create with those of your supporters with whom you choose to get **Married**. Supporters who reach this stage are likely to be not only some of your most enthusiastic advocates, but they will also be people whom you respect a great deal, are inspired by and with whom you may have developed a close friendship. At the Marriage stage, both of you will be sharing the investment, as you will be creating products together. In the musician example, at the Marriage stage you might be collaborating on an album or embarking on a tour together. You would both have a stake in the set-up costs and you would both be receiving a share of the eventual profits. The guidance on whom you choose to enter a marriage partnership with is to ensure that you are both bringing equivalent value to the table, otherwise there is the potential for conflict and imbalance as the partnership progresses.

The Harsh Truth

You want to know why there exists a common perception that it is nearly impossible to earn a decent living as an artist or performer? Because most artists or performers never even get beyond the Dating stage in terms of the products they offer their supporters. Since they've never even heard of a product pyramid, let alone used one, they are painfully ignorant (or all too painfully aware) of how difficult it is to keep house and home together. To see why this struggle exists, let's look at the suggested pricing structure for the Product Pyramid:

Product Level	Suggested Price Range
Courting	Free
Dating	Free - £100
Mating	£100 - £999
Relationship	£1000 - £3000
Living Together	£3000 - £5000
Engaged	£5000 - £10000
Married	Shared investment, shared profit

Albums, books, CDs, DVDs, T-shirts, prints, hoodies, caps: all of these products fall in the Dating price range. This means that unless you have at least 2000 supporters willing to buy at least one of these items from you once a year, you will struggle to bring home anything like the average UK household income of just over £20 000 a year, and that's before you've taken into account any of the costs of creating the product itself.

Even if you think your 'enough' may be significantly lower than that figure, it is important not to be blind to the double-edged sword the internet presents you with. True, the internet offers you a potential audience of millions and no end of ways to connect and communicate with your audience. However, the web offers that same audience almost as many ways to get your stuff for free. This is why it is so essential that you are evolving relationships with 'supporters', not just fans, and why you must be inspiring those supporters to invest in your gift to at least the Relationship level.

Fans vs Supporters

To understand the distinction between fans and supporters, let me use an example of someone I choose to support. I am a *fan* of a number of different Hip Hop artists. However, I am a big *supporter* of an artist called Immortal Technique. I value his passion and the controversial, yet highly informative content of his lyrics. I also value that he is independent of any corporate record label and that he has used the proceeds from his album sales to fund the building of an orphanage in Afghanistan. I know that any money I invest in supporting him will be used for the greater benefit of humankind. Therefore, even though I could get his stuff for free, I choose to buy his albums, documentary films, tickets to his shows and T-Shirts from his merchandise shop. **A supporter is someone who will choose to invest in what you are offering even when they could get it for free.**

The challenge you face is to be consistently coming up with engaging ways to attract such supporters and serve them through products that are highly valuable to them and highly rewarding to you. To help you kick-start this process, you can get creative with the Productise Me Plan in the Creative Uprising Playbook.

You and Your Movement

Now that you are aware of the level of support you'll need, the question is how are you going to attract such a significant and active group of supporters, whose love and loyalty runs so deep that they will be happy to buy what they could get for free?

The answer lies in proudly unfurling your banner. You must give your supporters something they can march behind. **You must create your movement**. TED Talks is a movement. Their mission – to share ideas worth spreading. Likewise,

Wikipedia, who want to make information freely accessible to anyone. If you feel that either of these organisations are doing work you consider important, you can join the community and start contributing. You must give your supporters the same opportunity.

Certainly, the time for movement-building is now. Simon Dixon revealed in his interview that the key to developing strong social capital is tribe-building, and that the essential ingredient of successful tribe building is to adopt a Pay It Forward approach:

> 'How you build your tribe and following is to be a friend to lots of people. We are still in a day and age where we can only manage a small number of close relationships, but we can manage lots and lots of small favours for people. The more small favours for people that you do, the higher your social capital is going to go. It's getting away from what you want, and figuring out how you can solve a lot of people's problems and doing small favours. The more of that you do, the more it will pay dividends in the future.'

The importance of Dixon's point cannot be overstated. If the opening of this section gave the impression that you are building your movement so that you will have supporters who will buy your stuff, let me dispel that notion now. The support you receive will be in direct proportion to the extent to which you serve others. Your movement is the vehicle for your gift to really serve. Thanks to the power of synergy, and in the same way that the accolades will follow if you get the mastery right, your movement will also be the most effective way to ensure you are rewarded as you deserve to be, but only if your focus is always on increasing your capacity to serve.

Defining Your Movement

Your movement will be defined by the values you live. Recall the 'Ethics' of your REAL strategy. Your supporters need to know what you stand for, so that they can align with you and champion you. Your movement must take into account the impact the rising culture is having. Within the next few years, if your efforts to earn a living are not also contributing to benefiting people or planet in some way, you will be seen, at best, as a dinosaur who can be ignored or, at worst, as a parasite who is despised. You need only bear witness to the growth of sites like Avaaz or to the viral spread of the KONY film to know how swiftly the world can now share issues it considers important. Make this phenomenon your friend, not your enemy.

Your movement will be built around how your gift empowers you and others to live the values you believe in. However, to draw people to your movement you will need a rallying cry: an inspiring message that makes people want to get on board. A good quotation to bear in mind when thinking about your rallying cry, comes from Simon Sinek, author of *Start with Why,* who suggests that, 'Poor leaders want others to follow them. Great leaders are committed to an idea or cause greater than themselves.'

A rousing Rallying Cry will accomplish three things:

1. It must tell people why you are doing what you do (it implicitly or explicitly states what you believe).

2. It must express a revolutionary new idea (or make an existing idea better).

3. It must communicate the greater cause you are committed to.

To show you this in action, I'll break down my rallying call for you: 'Do what you love. Give your Gift. Change the world.' The revolutionary idea is 'do what you love,' 'give your gift' contains my passionate belief that each person has a gift the world needs, and 'change the world' is the greater cause I am committed to.

Building Your Tribe

Now that you know how to attract people to your movement, we must consider how you can transform those who have enthusiastically answered your rallying cry into fully-fledged supporters and members of tribe 'you'. In short, there must be some clear benefits to getting on board with your movement. Even if they are not ready to go to the Relationship stage of your products yet, you should ensure they can choose from a number of Courting gifts and that, at the very least, they enjoy Dating whenever the chance arises. Remember you are a servant leader. Let them know you are grateful for their support, find out what else they want and find ways to give it to them.

There are two things to bear in mind when building your movement. Firstly, you are not trying to attract everyone. If you are the owner of a sweetshop, you do not want people coming in who want to buy guns. It would be a waste of time on both sides. Similarly, you are interested only in welcoming to your tribe those who are inspired by the gift you have to give the world, and who are passionate about seeing your rallying call becoming reality. Secondly, don't let the Creative Castrator of your ego fool you into thinking you're doing something arrogant or wrong in trying to build your movement. If you've ever liked a facebook page, subscribed to a YouTube channel or followed a twitter account, you've become part of a movement. You build yours however works best for you, but do it with passion and joy and in a way that inspires you, because that way you'll attract just the kinds of supporters you'd love to serve.

Creating your movement is such a vital part of how you rally supporters to you and how you give your gift in the fullest way. For this reason, I've put together an extensive 'Make Your Movement' section in the Creative Uprising Playbook, where you can devise your rallying call and define the movement that will define you.

CHAPTER 11

Performers Are The New Politicians

The Re-emergence of an Old Way

Before the printing press made the dissemination of information more widespread, and before Da Vinci and his peers were giving birth to the Renaissance, people relied on performers for their news and entertainment. Poets, minstrels, fools and troubadours are some of the titles given to the nomadic or patronised edutainers whose role was to entertain and amuse, whilst upholding and critiquing the social order and the actions of its rulers.

The role of the fool was particularly significant. In Shakespeare's King Lear, Goneril expresses her annoyance at the king's 'all-licensed fool'. This is a reference to the fact that the fool had a unique position within the medieval court that gave him/her license to upbraid the king or queen and hold them to account even as they entertained them.

These performers also had a vital role to play beyond the courts of nobility. In market squares of the towns and villages, where literacy was virtually unheard of beyond the clerical orders, the minstrels/jesters would champion the underdog, the everyman, lampooning authority figures and dispensing morality and social values wrapped up in laughter.

The World as a Stage

Today what constitutes a performer has evolved. Now, if you are publicly sharing your story, expressing a message or representing a cause, you are in the role of performer as it once was, able to influence opinion and contribute wisdom and insight where it is needed. There is great power in this and if you are prepared to accept the responsibility that goes with such power, the impact of your gift and your ability to serve will be greatly heightened.

Prior to the advent of the internet, it was much more of a challenge to spread ideas rapidly. The damage could be done before people had time to organise and prevent the kind of united front that might have prevented the perpetrators from proceeding with their perfidy. Today, however, in the space of 24 hours, millions of people can learn the truth about a situation, allowing them to swiftly instigate the appropriate response. I mentioned the KONY film earlier, and it really was a staggering example of how quickly a movement with a powerful rallying call can gain mass attention. It took just nine days from its release on March 14th 2012 for the film to reach 100 million views. What that equates to is that more than 128 people per second were watching the video during that period. That is a truly incredible response. Neither the questionable legitimacy of the film's intentions, nor the subsequent arrest of its creator can detract from what it proved: that the Creative Uprising has a leading role to play in shaping the governance of the rising culture. The world needs your gift, because when you give your gift you are being a courageous performer, and performers are the new politicians.

Meeting a Vital Need

When it comes to understanding why people like you have such a critical role to play in ensuring a future exists for the human race, you need look no further than The Iraq War of 2003. More than any other event of recent times, it devastated the Western world's ability to trust its political figures.

We made our feelings known through the largest anti-war protest in history, with some 10 million people marching the streets in cities throughout Europe and America. We then looked on in disgust as our collective voice was summarily ignored, whilst an already dodgy dossier was 'sexed up' and a brilliant scientist died in the most suspicious of circumstances.

The Obama era was ushered in with words the world so desperately wanted to be true: 'hope', 'change', 'believe.' We wanted to. We were so tired of corporate-funded politicians signing off the colonisation of the developing world. We wanted change we could believe in. Fast-forward to November 2012. America returned to the polls with people having little 'hope' and being reluctant to 'believe', because in the space of four years, there had been no 'change.' Most people now favoured Obama not because he offered them anything, but because he was just 'the lesser of two evils'.

In the void left by such disaffection and disenchantment, the world needs you to step up and embrace the important role you have. When the people of the world stop looking to political leaders for answers and guidance to the pressing challenges of the times, they will turn to leaders they do trust and respect – the servant leaders who are courageous enough to give their gift to the world by entertaining and informing the people who support them.

The Performer as Politician

In the late 1980s, gang related murders in American cities were claiming over 1000 young lives a year. To those ignorant of his deeper political efforts and opinions Tupac Shakur was the epitome of a violent, misogynistic thug rapper, whose lyrics contributed to the tide of death sweeping the streets. However, what is not widely known is that in 1992, Shakur hosted a 'Truce Picnic' where prominent members of the Bloods and the Crips (two of the most infamous warring gangs at the time) signed the 'Code of Thug Life', which was co-authored by Shakur and, among other directives, explicitly forbade the selling of drugs to pregnant women, the use of children as go-betweens in the drug trade and the selling of drugs outside schools. The signing of this code accelerated peace efforts, and in 1993 the Bloods and the Crips signed a truce pledging to end gang-related violence. Their actions sparked a peace movement that spread nationwide. Using his status as a well known performer, Shakur was able to have an influence on proceedings that no politicians or law enforcement officials had yet managed.

Ed Sheeran is another who has used his profile to actively champion a cause, a cause he feels rarely gets the support it deserves. In May 2012 Sheeran performed an intimate show in Bristol that raised £40 000 for the charity One25, which supports women trapped in sex work to break free from a life on the streets. This serves as a fantastic example of how embracing the role of performer as social leader can create amazing triple-win situations. Here, the charity benefited from the exposure and the money raised, the fans who participated in the fund-raising were rewarded with a fantastically rare intimate gig, and Ed was able to meet his need for contribution by serving a cause he passionately believed in.

Inspiring though both these examples are, perhaps none can touch the actions of Muhammad Ali, who sacrificed the best years of boxing career to go to jail in protest at the Vietnam war. The legacy he created through his courage and compassion will live as long in the hearts of humanity as any of his great victories. The challenges of today are far more insidious than the outright disgrace of the Vietnam draft. Corruption, poverty, climate change, scarcity of resources, ceaseless violence...the list of what we face could continue ad infinitum. There are no easy answers. What is certain, however, is that we are in the time of greatest need. It is a time when your friends, your family, your children's children need you to find in yourself a way to match Ali's courage and conviction and be the servant leader your supporters deserve.

The Consciously Gifted Leader

I understand it's possible you may by uncomfortable with the term 'leader'. Perhaps you are someone who naturally feels more comfortable in a support role, or maybe someone once told you weren't a natural leader and you chose to believe them. Whatever the reason might be, let me assure you that if you choose to be courageous enough to live your love and give the world your gift, then you are being a leader. You can't help it. How you choose to define yourself is entirely up to you, but, as you've already discovered, the very act of giving your gift is an act of service leadership.

And don't think you have to be influencing millions, unless you want to be. The instances documented above, or Immortal Technique's building of an orphanage in Afghanistan, are very public, very palpable examples of performers embracing the chance to be consciously gifted leaders. You may never wish to be that public. But, first and foremost, always, you are serving your supporters. That is what is means to be a consciously gifted leader – to be conscious of your supporters' needs and to be an exemplary servant leader by consistently sharing your gift in an attempt to enrich their lives.

Caring For Your Supporters

It is not necessary to be in their face all the time, insisting that they like this or share that. That's called being annoying, and has nothing to do with servant leadership. However else you choose to engage with your supporters, you must ensure you are doing the following:

1. Being your true, courageous self. This is why they became your supporter in the first place, and above and beyond anything else this is what you must always be. This is what first inspired your supporters to begin their journey with you and it is what will keep them marching to your banner and sharing your rallying cry.

2. Continually finding out what your supporters want and doing everything in your power to give it to them. This is what any government worth its salt should do, and it is what you must do if you are to best help yourself by helping your supporters.

To help you uncover the deep needs of your supporters you'll find the 'Support Your Supporter Profile' in the Creative Uprising Playbook a valuable resource to keep checking in with.

The Coopetition Key

Upon discovering your supporters' needs, you may realise you are unable to fully meet them under your own steam alone, and will therefore have to turn to others in your field for support. Rather than perceiving this as a sign of weakness or failure, embrace this as a fantastic opportunity to experience the power of Coopetition. Coopetition is the synergy of Competition and Cooperation and is an essential element of the rising culture.

Coopetition can best be summed up by the idea that you compete as individuals to help each other collectively. Each person within the field of a domain is competing with themselves and others to set new standards, but collectively all members of the field are cooperating to enhance the contributions of the entire domain as fully as possible.

The domain of Hip Hop culture always struck me as one of the best examples of this. Upon finishing university I made a decision that changed my life amazingly. I committed to becoming a UK Hip Hop entrepreneur, despite having no experience of either UK Hip Hop or entrepreneurship. Despite the fact that my friends were all heading off to get 'proper jobs', I decided to dive into what inspired me and, of course, the universe supported me. Within two months of finishing my final exams my team and I were hosting the first ever UK Hip Hop club-night in our local area. Over the next three years we immersed ourselves in a scene that was rapidly gaining popularity but which was struggling for mainstream recognition. The result of this dichotomy was a lack of places for this burgeoning art form to express itself. By providing a space where Emcees and DJs could show their skills, we were meeting a real need. As a result, at each new night we hosted there would be many rival crews in attendance and the competition on stage was fierce. However, out in the crowd and in the towns of the local area there was an amazing collective desire to see the scene we were nurturing be successful. If we needed a hand putting up flyers or posters, or were missing a piece of equipment, we only had to make a few phone calls and we would have many hands willing to help.

In reality, the people helping us were our competitors – we'd both have been trying to outdo each other if the chance to perform a stadium show had presented itself. However, our rivals understood that if they were to develop and thrive in the long term, a healthy local club scene was essential. Therefore they were committed to ensuring our club-nights were successful even at the same time as they tried to prove they were the number one artist/crew in the area.

Possible Futures

If the indications of the rising culture do play out into reality, coopetition will be one of the foundation stones on which a very different future is built. But what might that future look like? What might emerge in the next five, ten, fifty years, and how will it impact the world we know? Within the farthest extent of that time frame it is estimated that we will pass the singularity point, which is the point at which the intelligence of machines will surpass that of human beings.

Futurist and inventor Raymond Kurzweil, who has written extensively on this subject, suggests that the rapid progress being made in the fields of genetics, robotics and nanotechnology will fundamentally rewrite our conceptions of what it means to be human. Certainly the next five years will see augmented reality and 3-D printing become commonplace influences in our lives.

As we already discovered through Simon Dixon's insights, our relationship with money will be dramatically transformed. However, this won't just have an impact on you as an individual. Dixon believes the changes will have a huge impact on both a social and global level:

> 'We'll see a big, big shift towards funding socially, environmentally, value-creating things as opposed to pure consumerism and socially destructive things. When you're assessing purely on profit and credit rating that's what you'll get. When you're assessing based on social capital and transparency, you'll see a lot more things funded where the social values are high.'

What does this mean for you? The advance of technology, as we have already experienced, will present challenges as well as opportunities. Part of performing your gift will be to keep abreast of and digest the changes occurring and feed back to your supporters how the changes will affect your movement and how you and they can collectively prosper as a result of what the changes bring about.

Blessings, Curses and Belonging

In considering the inevitable growth and impact of technology, it is vital to maintain a balanced perspective. Without doubt, the reach, connectivity and abundance of resources offered by technology must be considered a blessing toward you giving your gift in the fullest possible way. However, without an awareness of the potential curses that accompany our advance into an ever more digitised world, there is a great danger that something irrevocable will be lost: our sense of belonging.

Technology apparently lets us connect with one another like never before, but the richness of our ability to connect cannot mask the poverty of the connection itself. Even for all that Skype can allow us to see and hear our friends as we converse with them, we cannot truly connect with someone unless they are face to face. We are not truly sharing laughter if we cannot see the joy dancing in the person's eyes as they laugh their unique laugh, a laugh that arrives at our ears undiluted by compressors, microphones and fibre-optic cables. Technology will become a curse if we allow it to become a substitute for real, alive, present human connection.

The Art of Belonging

Real human connection depends on maintaining what Alastair McIntosh, founder of the Centre for Human Ecology and author of *Soil & Soul: The People vs Corporate Power*, calls 'the cycle of belonging,' which concerns 'the way that place, values and human identity join up to find expression'. At its heart, the cycle of belonging is about staying connected to the natural world, to the land, and honouring the interdependence of the work and community which the land sustains.

It is this connection that is perhaps most endangered by the ubiquity of the online world, and when we lose this, according to McIntosh, we lose our 'traction with life', because our communities become no longer communities of place, where soil, soul and society harmoniously enrich each other and we are able to interact with the fullness of life's challenges, boons and mysteries. It is for this reason, perhaps, that McIntosh's immediate response, when asked how the creative arts could influence social and environmental change, was, 'Get grounded...let the force of nature shape you into a force of nature. Do your art from a place where you are connected with the community, with the earth.'

Finding Balance

One thing that is sure is that if we come to rely too heavily on the advance of technology and allow it to erode our connection with each other and with the planet that ultimately sustains us all, then the rising culture will fall just as quickly as it has risen and the future of humanity will certainly not be assured. But that is why you are reading this now, so you can serve and empower your people and your planet by giving the incredible gift that you are mastering. To stand out in your field, to lead the way, you must serve. Your gift is the greatest service you can do. The rising culture is the shift from surviving to thriving and you are central to it. As Alastair McIntosh so passionately put it in an article for *The Guardian* newspaper, 'Politics, economics and technology on their own are not enough. We must also tackle the roots of consumerism, consumption in excess of sufficiency – the idolatrous addiction that masks our inner emptiness and poisons deeper transformation. And so we must rekindle community, put love back into public life, and thereby rescue hope from the caverns of despair. We must call back the soul.'

When you do what brings you alive, and make the effort each day to master and share your gift in ever more brilliant ways, you honour the urge of your soul and by doing so serve as an inspiring example for others to do the same. Your act of courage actively contributes to the emergence of a life that is more whole, more nourishing, more energising and alive.

A Final Invitation

As we arrive at the end of our journey, it occurs to me that I might owe you an apology of sorts. I have poured my heart and soul into putting this book together, in the hope that it will help you to help yourself as you help others. But perhaps there have been times when I have gone against my own sound advice. Perhaps there have been moments where I have held back from saying all that I would truly wish to say, so as not to sound 'a too bit much' or 'a bit over the top'. In these final few paragraphs, let me uncensor myself.

The truth is: you are a miracle. A living, breathing source of infinite brilliance and it is a humbling honour that you have taken the time to appreciate this book. With everything I am, I hope you will never lose sight of how amazing you are.

There has never been a being, in the whole history and future of the cosmos, who can offer life what you can offer. Therefore, it is your absolute right to feel love and joy and gratitude in boundless abundance. Nothing and no one can rob you of that. Never forget you are so powerful! Your every thought, feeling, word and deed leaves an indelible mark on the very fabric of existence, so make your mark one that inspires beyond this time and place, that leaves an exponential legacy of love to nourish all life.

You are the Creative Uprising. Your Reason is your bliss, your Purpose is to do what brings you alive without compromise or fear, to dare to become what you only ever dreamt of being.

I invite you to celebrate each new self-discovery, to devotedly develop your mastery and to deliver, with unwavering commitment, your unique contribution to life.

I invite you to give your gift.

References:

Chapter 1:

Anthony Robbins – Human Needs
http://www.ted.com/talks/tony_robbins_asks_why_we_do_what_we_do.html.

Flow
Csikszentmihalyi, Mihaly *Flow: The Science of Optimal Experience.* Harper Perennial (2005).

Goethe quote
http://www.goethesociety.org/pages/quotescom.html.

Jim Rohn Quote
http://www.google.co.uk/url?sa=t&rct=j&q=&esrc=s&source=web&cd=9&sqi=2&ved=0CGEQFjAI&url=http%3A%2F%2Fwww.jimrohn.com%2Fimages%2Fuploads%2FCGW_pillar2.pdf&ei=W1wIUbK3HNL02wX2_oH4BQ&usg=AFQjCNGXuEL1vzSGUbt4i-mvCo24sKQbsA&bvm=bv.41642243,d.b2I.

Chapter 2:

Laszlo, Ervin.
Science and the Reenchantment of the Cosmos. Inner Traditions (2006).

Emoto, Masaru
The Hidden Messages in Water. Pocket Books (2005).

Rawson, Frederick L.
Life Understood: From a Scientific and Religious Point of View. Cosimo Classics (2007).

Wilcock, David
The Source Field Investigations.
Penguin (2011).

Steve Jack – interview conducted for this book

Mascaro, Juan (trans)
The Bhagavad Gita.
Penguin Classics (2003).

Brené Brown on courage and vulnerability
http://www.ted.com/talks/brene_brown_on_vulnerability.
html.

Marianne Williamson Quote
Williamson, Marianne, *A Return to Love.* Thorsons (1996).

'What if' Walk adapted from:
http://danielpriestley.wordpress.com/2012/08/15/what-to-
do-if-you-are-doing-it-tough

Chapter 3:

Chris Hughes – Interview conducted for this book

Affluence diagram inspired by
Robin, Vicki
Your Money or Your Life.
Penguin (2008).

Chapter 4:

Chapter 5:

Ed Sheeran info
http://en.wikipedia.org/wiki/Ed_Sheeran.

http://www.4music.com/news/news/7422/Ed-Sheerans-The-A-Team-goes-platinum-in-US.

Practice

Coyle, Daniel
The Talent Code: Greatness isn't born, it's Grown.
Arrow Books (2010).

Ericsson, K. Anders
The Danger of Delegating Education to Journalists: Why the APS Observer Needs Peer Review When Summarizing New Scientific Developments
Letter to APS Observer (2012).

Ericsson, K. A., & Towne, T. J.
Experts and their superior performance.
In D. M. Reisberg, (Ed.), The Oxford Handbook of Cognitive Psychology. New York, NY: Oxford University Press, Inc. (2013).

Mindset

http://www.bedfordshire-news.co.uk/Sport/Cricket/Cricket-Bedford-School-use-Alastair-Cook-recipe-20121210095936.htm

http://www.espncricinfo.com/wisdencricketer/content/story/250165.html

Setting

Syed, Matthew
Bounce: The Myth of Talent and the Power of Practice
Fourth Estate

Other info

Chapter 6:

Ronaldo info

http://soccerlens.com/stat-attack-the-relentless-cristiano-ronaldo/79143/

http://www.dailymail.co.uk/sport/football/article-511586/Practice-makes-Mr-Perfect-Ronaldo.html.

Cantona info

http://blogs.telegraph.co.uk/sport/markogden/100023597/how-eric-cantona-changed-english-football-forever-20-years-ago-today/.

Craig Johnston info

http://www.telegraph.co.uk/sport/football/7346219/Ive-had-a-bit-of-a-rough-time-but-Im-still-here-says-former-Liverpool-star-Craig-Johnston.html

http://www.guardian.co.uk/football/2004/jan/08/newsstory.sport3.

Deliberate practice

Ericsson, K. Anders, Prietula, Michael J., and Cokely, Edward T.
The Making of an Expert
Harvard Business Review (July–August 2007).

Tiger woods info

http://www.thegolfblog.com/2011/04/the-golf-blog-why-tiger-woods-swing-change-is-admission-of-mistake-in-leaving-butch-harmon.html

http://en.wikipedia.org/wiki/Tiger_Woods.

Mastery Curve – adapted from:

Leonard, George.
Mastery: The Keys to Success and Long-term Fulfilment.
Plume (1992).

Chapter 7:

Anti-social Monkeys

http://www.psychologytoday.com/blog/games-primates-play/201203/what-monkeys-can-teach-us-about-human-behavior-facts-fiction.

Socialisation

Csikszentmihalyi, Mihaly
Flow: The Science of Optimal Experience
Harper Perennial (2005)

Child well being

http://www.ipce.info/newsletters/e_22/2_10_unicef_report.htm.

Suicide

http://www.bbc.co.uk/news/uk-17325174.

Jim Rohn quote

http://personalexcellence.co/blog/101-most-inspiring-quotes-part-4/.

Masterminding

Pearsall, Karl and Attram, Mac:
www.Masterminding.net

Schwarzenegger interview

Empire Magazine
Bauer Consumer Media (October 2012)

Chapter 8:

Tyson Gay interview

http://www.thenewsmarket.com/Assets/PrintFriendly_
assetDetails.aspx?GUID=c000b3d2-4c46-4d5a-a581-
a5bb2b899a08&Screen=PRINT-FRIENDLY&Page=Print.

Chapter 9:

Football trainee figures

http://www.telegraph.co.uk/sport/2425278/Football-
trainees-may-have-to-learn-the-hard-way.html.

Drama school application figures

http://www.thestudentroom.co.uk/showthread.
php?t=996399.

Queans Restaurant

http://www.telegraph.co.uk/foodanddrink/
restaurants/9259827/Queans-Leamington-Spa-restaurant-
review.html.

Sandi Thom

http://en.wikipedia.org/wiki/Sandi_Thom.

http://www.streamingtank.com/clients/list/sandi-thom/.

Impact of positive thinking on brain chemistry

Heard in a talk by Brian Mayne at the 2012 UK Youth Leadership Summit

Choosing an empowering meaning

Singha, Harry
Light up Your Life: An inspirational guide on turning your worst days into your best days
Light Up Your Life Press (2011)

Chapter 10:

Advanced indigenous cultures

Hartmann, Thomas
The Last hours of Ancient Sunshine: Revised and Updated: The Fate of the World and What We Can Do Before It's Too Late
Broadway Books (2001)

Poverty stats:

http://www.globalissues.org/article/26/poverty-facts-and-stats.

Arms stats:

http://www.stwr.org/food-security-agriculture/us-30-billion-a-year-would-eradicate-world-hunger.html.

http://www.freethechildren.com/international-programming/our-model/education/.

Simon Dixon

Interview conducted for this book

Polly A. Bauer

Stats from a presentation given at the Mission Profitable conference in 2012

Priestley, Daniel *Become a Key Person of Influence: The Five-Step Sequence to becoming one fo the most highly valued and highly paid people in your industry* Ecademy Press.

Simon Dixon quote

Interview conducted for this book.

Simon Sinek Quote

https://twitter.com/simonsinek/status/290953844005933056.

Sinek, Simon
Start With Why
Penguin (2011).

Chapter 11:

Shakepseare, William
King Lear
Arden (1997).

Iraq War protest figures

http://mobilizingideas.wordpress.com/category/essay-dialogues/the-iraq-war-protests-10-years-later/.

Tupac Shakur

http://www.mutulushakur.com/thuglife.html.

http://www.finalcall.com/artman/publish/National_News_2/article_8843.shtml.

Ed Sheeran One25 campaign

http://www.bbc.co.uk/news/uk-england-bristol-18163708.

Raymond Kurzweil

http://transcendentman.com/.

Alastair McIntosh

Interview conducted for this book, plus:

http://www.alastairmcintosh.com/articles/2008-phd-thesis-alastair-mcintosh-web.pdf.

http://www.guardian.co.uk/commentisfree/belief/2009/oct/03/climate-change-economy-quakers-piscator.

http://www.guardian.co.uk/commentisfree/belief/2011/oct/21/hope-art-wassily-kandinsky-relevant.

Resources:

You can find an updated list at CreativeUprising.com/Resources

Discover:

Non-Fiction Books:

The Divine Matrix: Bridging Time, Space, Miracles and Belief
By Gregg Bradden

Science and the Reenchantment of the Cosmos: The Rise of the Integral Vision of Reality
By Ervin Laszlo

Now Discover Your Strengths: How to Develop Your Talents and Those of the People You Manage
By Marcus Buckingham and Donald O. Clifton

The Daemon: A Guide to Your Extraordinary Secret Self
By Anthony Peake

The Field: The Quest for the Secret Force of the Universe
By Lynn McTaggert

The Element: How Finding Your Passions Changes Everything
By Ken Robinson

The Hidden Science of Lost Civilisations: The Source Field Investigations
By David Wilcock

Fingerprints of the Gods: The Quest Continues
By Graham Hancock

Fiction and Poetry:

Gitanjali
By Rabindranath Tagore

The Prophet
By Kahlil Gibran

Aghora 1, 2 & 3
By Robert E. Svoboda

Films

What the Bleep do we Know?
Directed by William Arntz, Betsy Chase and Mark Vicente

The Secret
Directed by Drew Heriot

The Peaceful Warrior
Directed by Victor Salva

Develop:

Non-Fiction Books:

Mastery: The Keys to Success and Long-Term Fulfillment
By George Leonard

The Making of an Expert
By K Anders Ericsson, Michael J. Prietula and Edward T. Cokely

(Published in the Harvard Business Review)
The Talent Code: Greatness isn't Born. It's Grown.
By Daniel Coyle

Bounce: The Myth of Talent and the Power of Practice
By Matthew Syed

Living Your Best Year Ever
By Darren Hardy

If You Want to Write: A Book about Art, Independence and Spirit
By Brenda Ueland

Deliver:

Entrepreneur Revolution: How to Develop Your Entrepreneurial Mindset and Start a Business That Works
By Daniel Priestley

Start With Why: How Great Leaders Inspire Everyone To Take Action
By Simon Sinek

The Four Hour Work Week: Escape the 9-5, Live Anywhere and Join the New Rich
By Tim Ferris

The Work We Were Born To Do
By Nick Williams

About George Hardwick

George is an inspiring poet, performer, speaker and teacher who uses creativity and the power of language to help people and organisations connect to their true purpose.

Alongside regular performances at Glastonbury festival, George has shared the stage with Sir Richard Branson, has rap-battled Ed Sheeran, and has performed his poetry on four continents and to TV audiences in excess of 7 million people.

Whether speaking from the stage, hosting group work, or in his role as a one-to-one mentor, George shares how the principles of what he terms 'The Creative Uprising', can help people to live more fulfilled lives whilst making a profound difference to the world we live in.

George's home is the beautiful English county of Warwickshire, where he lives with his wife and daughter. He spends his free time cooking, writing, playing sport and immersing himself in community projects.

If you would like to learn more about The Creative Uprising, head over to www.CreativeUprising.com, where you can access educational resources, interviews and the Creative Uprising Community. Alternatively, if you would like to connect with George, or discover more about his work as a performer, speaker, trainer and mentor, visit www.GeorgeHardwick.com or drop an email to Connect@GeorgeHardwick.com

Notes:

Notes:

Notes:

Notes:

Notes:

Notes: